BIM and 3D GIS Integration for Digital Twins

Building information modelling (BIM) uses a combination of technologies and resources to capture, manage, analyse, and display a digital representation of the physical and functional characteristics of a facility. A Geographic Information System (GIS) offers tools for visualising and analysing built and natural environments and their impacts on infrastructure systems, such as land use, transportation, etc. This book offers a framework for how the geospatial and surveying industry can create and integrate BIM with GIS. Through practical implementation methods, readers will learn to merge GIS data with design and BIM data to enable digital twins.

This book presents the following features:

- Integrates BIM and GIS from a geospatial and surveying point of view for the first time;
- Addresses the creation of BIM from existing constructed buildings instead of typical pre-construction scenarios;
- Explains how to deliver BIM-suitable surveys to surveyors and geospatial practitioners;
- Provides surveying and geospatial industry expertise in the collecting, locating, managing, and communicating of BIM;
- Introduces new knowledge on the validation and integration of BIM and GIS within the spatial industry.

This is an excellent book for professionals working with 3D data for built-environment digital twins, such as city planners, land surveyors, and geospatial practitioners. It is also an insightful resource for those working and studying in the fields of GIS, surveying, and geospatial engineering, providing the most current tools and resources for dealing with BIM.

BIM and 3D GIS Integration for Digital Twins

An Introduction

Mohsen Kalantari, Christian Clemen,
and Mojgan Jadidi

CRC Press is an imprint of the
Taylor & Francis Group, an **informa** business

Designed cover image: Shutterstock

First edition published 2025
by CRC Press
2385 NW Executive Center Drive, Suite 320, Boca Raton FL 33431

and by CRC Press
4 Park Square, Milton Park, Abingdon, Oxon, OX14 4RN

CRC Press is an imprint of Taylor & Francis Group, LLC

ISBN: 978-0-8153-9175-3 (hbk)
ISBN: 978-1-032-89378-5 (pbk)
ISBN: 978-1-351-20095-0 (ebk)

DOI: 10.1201/9781351200950

Typeset in Palatino
by Newgen Publishing UK

To Ailar, Aiden, Alma, and my parents (Mohsen Kalantari).

To Amytis, Kyarash, my sisters, and my parents (Mojgan Jadidi).

To Jana, Joris, Elisabeth, and my parents (Christian Clemen).

Contents

Preface

For over a decade, alongside many esteemed colleagues worldwide, we have been undertaking research and development in the nexus of 3D geographic information systems (GIS) and building information modelling (BIM). While there is a rich body of knowledge within research papers and edited books, no textbooks outline and link the fundamentals of BIM and GIS integration (such as the theory of 3D modelling, creating BIM using geospatial methods, georeferencing BIM, and steps to integrate BIM into GIS) or how these data sources can be the foundation for creating digital twins of built environments.

Knowledge in existing research papers is often time-sensitive and narrow. Researchers target them not to learn the fundamentals but to see what is cutting-edge. Cutting-edge research will further improve BIM and GIS integration, but what remains the same is the fundamental science and engineering underpinning BIM and GIS and enabling their integration for the creation of digital twins.

We have authored a unique book that offers the fundamental concepts of BIM and GIS integration in a coherent and organised manner. Our focus is not just the theory but also the practical application of these concepts. We specifically target researchers who are new to BIM and GIS integration, tertiary educators, coursework students, and practitioners in surveying, geospatial, and architecture, engineering, and construction (AEC) disciplines. These groups will be able to use our book as a textbook covering the fundamentals of 3D modelling in GIS, the basics of BIM, practical steps to create BIM using geospatial and surveying methods, and the practical challenges in integrating BIM into GIS from the perspective of the foundation of digital twins development.

This book will help readers to learn the basics of 3D GIS modelling and BIM and how to create and use BIM in 3D GIS, all within the broader field of digital twins. This book delves deep into the technical aspects of creating BIM and integrating it into 3D GIS for built-environment applications.

In Chapter 1, the book discusses why BIM and GIS integration matters in the context of digital twins for city planning, development, and management, emphasising the role of BIM and GIS within broader smart city frameworks. Chapter 2 delves into the theory of 3D data models, storage, and visualisation, discussing alternatives that are relevant to BIM and 3D GIS. Chapter 3 introduces the fundamentals of BIM and its benefits beyond construction, presenting relevant standards and analysis tools. Chapter 4 discusses methodologies for creating BIM for existing buildings and infrastructure using geospatial and surveying techniques. Chapter 5 addresses the various levels and methods of georeferencing BIM. Chapter 6 focuses on integrating BIM and 3D GIS, including relevant methodologies and standards. Chapter 7 concludes by formalising the definition of digital twins in the context of built environments, identifying the importance of digital twins for effective decision-making in built environments and highlighting the need for multi-disciplinary skills, such as BIM and GIS, for the digital transformation of cities.

About the Authors

Mohsen Kalantari is an Associate Professor of Geospatial Engineering at the School of Civil and Environmental Engineering and a co-founder of the Scan-to-BIM technology start-up Faramoon. His research interests include land administration, 3D cadastres, 3D GIS, and BIM. He has previously worked for the Department of Infrastructure Engineering at the University of Melbourne. Before his academic career, he worked in the surveying and spatial industry as the Victorian Coordinator of a nationwide land and survey information modernisation initiative (ePlan) in Australia.

Christian Clemen has been a full Professor of BIM and Surveying at the School of Geospatial Information, University of Applied Sciences Dresden, Germany (HTWD), since 2013. He has previously worked as a trained surveying technician in an engineering office, a researcher at the Technical University of Berlin, and a software developer for GNSS real-time systems, as well as completing his PhD. In addition to teaching, Christian is actively involved in standardisation (DIN/CEN/ISO/buildingSMART). For over two decades, he has been engaged in the 3D information modelling of buildings and the semantic integration of the AEC and geospatial domains, always from the perspective of surveying practice.

Mojgan Jadidi is an Associate Professor of Civil Engineering at the Lassonde School of Engineering, York University, Canada. Her research interests include the development of digital twins by integrating BIM, GIS, and sensor data; geospatial visual analytics; and spatial quantum computing for the application of smart environments, buildings, infrastructure, and cities. She founded the Geospatial Visual Analytics (GeoVA) Lab, where she passionately drives research in cutting-edge technology development for safer and more resilient built environments. She also lends her technical expertise to the classroom, providing immersive learning experiences using virtual and augmented reality and gamification technologies for engineering education.

1

Why Do Digital Twins Matter?

1.1 The World Population Will Still Grow but at a Slower Pace

People are at the centre of development; therefore, understanding how populations change is fundamental to social stability, environmental sustainability, and the economic prosperity of the world.

In mid-November 2022, the world accommodated almost 8 billion inhabitants. The world population was 6.6 billion in 2005, meaning that the world's population increased by 1.4 billion people in 17 years. The vast majority (60%) of people live in Asia, while Africa accommodates 17%, Europe hosts 10%, Latin America and the Caribbean accommodate 9%, and the rest of the population resides in North America and Oceania. The global population is projected to increase to 9.7 billion by 2050, with a potential peak approaching nearly 10.4 billion in the mid-2080s (Baker et al., 2023), meaning that the population will continue grow but at a slower pace. In the last 10 years, the growth rate has been about 1.24% per year, but this rate will decline slightly to 1.10% per year.

As the world's population increases, it is essential to understand how it will be distributed in urban and rural regions.

1.2 Urbanisation is a Global Phenomenon

The share of global city populations has doubled from 25% in 1950 to approximately 50% in 2020. It is anticipated to rise gradually to 58% over the next 50 years (Khor et al., 2022).

Between 2020 and 2070, the number of cities in low-income countries is expected to increase by 76%, while cities in high-income and lower middle-income countries are expected to increase by around 20% and those in upper middle-income countries by 6% (Khor et al., 2022).

In the next five decades, the expansion of city land areas will primarily occur in low-income (141%), lower middle-income (44%), and high-income

DOI: 10.1201/9781351200950-1

countries (34%). Changes in upper middle-income countries are projected to be relatively modest (13%) (Khor et al., 2022).

Small cities currently occupy nearly half of city land areas (about 45%) in low-income countries and this trend is expected to persist in the coming decades (Khor et al., 2022).

The concentration of populations in urban areas means that urban and territorial planning tools are essential for mitigating the adverse social, economic, and environmental impacts associated with future urban growth. This is particularly critical for low-income nations and they must have the tools to be able to carefully plan to prevent undue pressure on existing open land, infrastructure, and services.

1.3 Cities as Economic Engines

While having most of the world's population living in cities presents challenges for development, it is vital to note the advantages of cities. Cities are regarded as efficient systems that bring about productivity and competitiveness. Due to the population concentration and more people interacting and communicating with each other, cities are the centre of knowledge, innovation, and learning. Cities are also bigger marketplaces, boosting trade and commerce. The larger populations help with efficiency and productivity. Cities drive cultural, social, technological, and political advancements (Bertinelli & Black, 2004; Bettencourt et al., 2007; Colenbrander, 2016).

It is evident that the economies of countries cannot grow without the growth of cities. Cities contribute significantly more than rural areas. Indeed, they generate 80% of the global GDP. There are several factors that contribute to the growth of cities, including geographical location and natural advantages, knowledge centres, industries, trades, infrastructure, and political significance. These factors help to attract businesses, workers, and consumers to cities (UN-Habitat, 2011).

It has also been proven that cities help with poverty reduction. In some Asian countries, the average income of the urban population is more than that of the rural population. For example, by implementing urbanisation policies, China has removed 220 million people from poverty in less than 25 years. This is also evident in the US, where the poverty rate is five times higher in rural areas than urban areas (UN-Habitat, 2011).

A significant amount of wealth is also generated in cities by creating new land and business-friendly environments. Governments capture the value of land by purchasing land, reselling it, and introducing different types of taxes on land. The captured value is then invested in urban development and infrastructure. The economic power of cities is attributed to the level of productivity, capital intensity, human capital, and the density of infrastructure, such as transport, communication, power supply, water and sanitation, housing, and financial and business services.

1.4 Smarter Management of Cities

As more and more of the global population becomes concentrated in cities, the need for initiatives and concepts that shape cities into better places to live and work increases. The concept of a smart city is one of the fundamental terminologies used in these kinds of initiatives. There is no standard definition of a smart city, but rather, it is an umbrella term for a wide range of city-related concepts. This includes concepts such as wired cities, virtual cities, ubiquitous cities, intelligent cities, information cities, digital cities, smart communities, knowledge cities, learning cities, sustainable cities, and green cities.

The term "smart city" also covers several dimensions of cities, including technological, human, and institutional dimensions. The technology dimension is about the use of information and communication technologies to transform the ways in which current cities operate and the ways in which people live and work in them. The human dimension is about social inclusiveness, learning, education, and knowledge. The institutional dimension is about the policy and governance of cities, by which stakeholders in cities, communities, and governments have the common goal of making cities a better place to live.

Most relevant to the topic of this book is the concept of digital twins, which refers to live digital representations and manifestations of built environments. We will talk about this concept in the next section. To better understand smart cities and their sub-concepts, particularly digital twins, it is essential to look at the drivers of smart cities.

The smart city concept emerged as a result of two major events: One was the global consensus on the need to reduce CO_2 (the Kyoto Protocol) and the other was the Internet becoming more accessible to the public (Cocchia, 2014). Following these events, we have observed an institutional recognition of the need to protect the environment by regulating and developing technology to make cities more efficient in terms of transport, urban planning, etc.

In this context, IBM's smart planet concept and the covenants of the Mayors of Europe have had influential roles in the development of the smart city concept. IBM's leadership in the smart planet concept is rooted in the competencies required to provide smarter services to have a good quality of life and make cities a better place to live. Building on this concept, IBM has started to develop new solutions for communication, transport, health, energy, and retail. The covenants of the Mayors of Europe have focused on the smart city concept and reducing CO_2 emissions by more than 20% by 2020 via actions targeting clean mobility, the redevelopment of buildings, and raising citizen awareness of energy consumption (Cocchia, 2014).

While these external drivers have pushed cities towards the smart concept, the theoretical framework of smart cities is far broader than simply environmental protection and technology adoption. What is more pronounced in theory is that smart cities need to be a better place to live. The theoretical framework of smart cities consists of several layers (Zygiaris, 2013; Figure 1.1): Layer 1, which includes the city and its governance, infrastructure, planning, and community; Layer 2 includes the communication infrastructure, wi-fi, broadband, 4G, and fibre network, which are technical matters; Layer 3 involves the instrumentation (i.e., sensors, RFID, and IoT) used to capture the events in the city in real time, which is, again, an economic and technical matter; Layer 4 is about the open integration of predominantly geospatially enabled data, which faces the issues of data heterogeneity and inconsistency and is where the use of ontologies, semantic systems, and linked APIs is pronounced; Layer 5 is the application layer where specific city matters are addressed, including energy, transport, democracy, government services, and homes; Layer 6 is the final layer and is concerned with innovation regarding how cities can be transformed using new business models that help with the growth of cities and the quality of life of their citizens.

1.5 Digital Twins and How They Fit into Smart Cities

As mentioned earlier, digital twins of cities are virtual and live representations of cities. Going back to the layers described above, one could argue that digital twins are realised by integrating Layers 3–5 of smart cities, whereby the communication, instrumentation, and data layers come together. Geospatial data are integral to digital twins and are where instrumentations and activities are localised. Geospatial data are often accessed through spatial data infrastructures (SDIs), which are set up for cities or broader jurisdictions to which cities belong. Geospatial data are organised in discrete thematic and application layers, which are linked via a common geospatial framework involving coordination and project systems. Historically, most of the

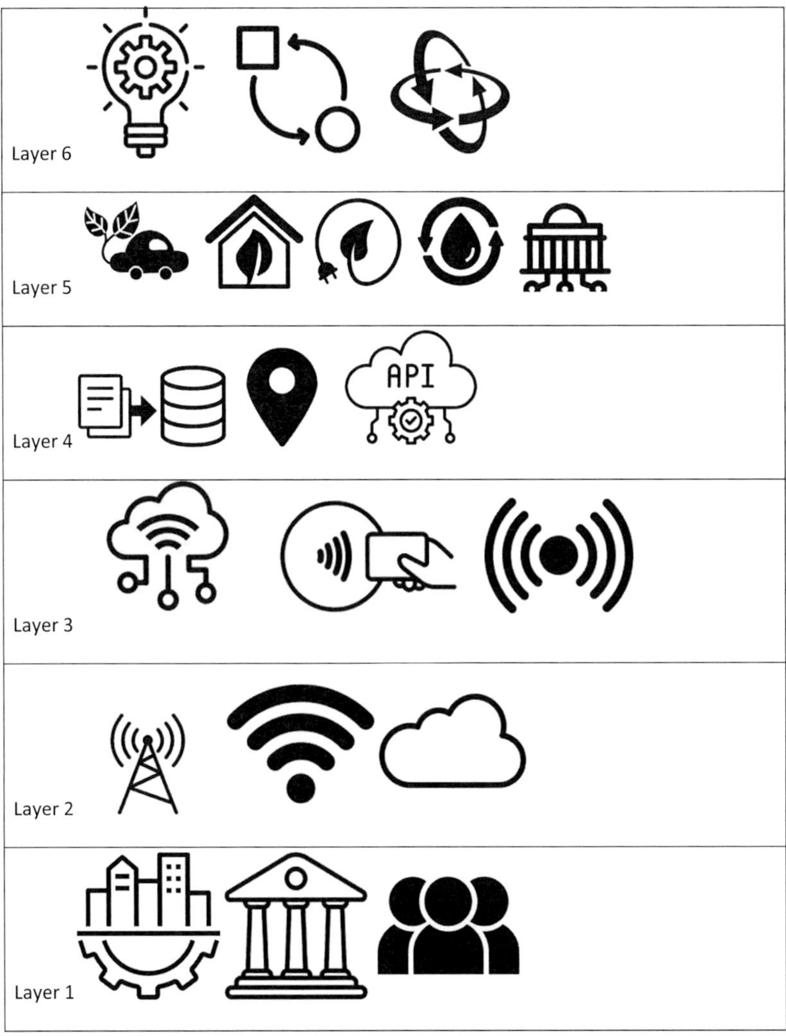

FIGURE 1.1
The conceptual model of components underpinning a smart city. (Adopted from Zygiaris, 2013.)

geospatial data in SDIs only involve 2D information. The notion of digital twins, though, involves an integrated view of the geospatial data of cities, with an emphasis on the third dimension of height and realistic representations of cities in a virtual environment. In digital twins, these representations are also expected to go beyond geometrical representations of built environments and, indeed, include live knowledge of cities via sensing technologies.

Digital twins are enormously valuable in various types of use cases in cities, including the following:

1. An environment to study the behaviour of residents and visitors of cities. As cities depend on their residents and visitors to survive, their experience is fundamental to cities' survival and digital twins can be leveraged to study, model, and predict people's behaviours in cities (Dembski et al., 2019);
2. A system to enable informed planning. Using digital twins, we can simulate alternatives by modifying, removing, and adding infrastructure within urban environments, which could help with better decision-making (Barresi, 2023; Ferré-Bigorra et al., 2022; Schrotter & Hürzeler, 2020);
3. Depicting environmental qualities. Urban qualities, such as heat islands, are abstract concepts driven by human and natural factors in cities. These qualities can be depicted using digital twins. The more spatial details and granularity that are available, the more accurate the representation of these qualities. Digital twins can assist with a better understanding of the complexities of urban environmental qualities (Qi et al., 2022; Ricciardi & Callegari, 2023; Tang et al., 2023);
4. Connecting people and built environments. Sensing infrastructure, such as the Internet of Things (IoT), is used to measure various phenomena across cities and provide services that matter to individual needs. At the same time, to address privacy concerns, people need to know where these sensing devices are and what functions or services they provide. Digital twins can be used to better understand the patterns of interconnections between people to design people-focused smart cities (Musse et al., 2019; Kismul et al., 2023; Samanta et al., 2022);
5. A metaverse. Digital twins have even been taken to the next level, wherein one can develop business opportunities and generate income at the cross-section of virtual and physical environments (Banaeian Far & Imani Rad, 2022; Jagatheesaperumal et al., 2023; Ko & Lee, 2022; Lv et al., 2022; Mourtzis, 2023). The visual representation of the real world in the metaverse is one example, i.e., one can develop a computer in Dell's virtual 3D spatial factory and then purchase it in the real world (Papagiannidis et al., 2008);
6. A practice arena for learning skills. Digital twins can be used for adults and children to practise and learn skills. In particular, these environments can provide people with learning disabilities the chance to freely explore the environment of a city and practice a variety of

living skills (Alves et al., 2022; Beheshti et al., 2023; Svelec et al., 2020; Tacchino et al., 2023; Vildjiounaite et al., 2023);

7. Cultural functions of cities. Cities have already benefited from virtual models in terms of culture and heritage. Advances in 3D modelling have benefited the cultural aspects of cities. Virtual environments provide means by which the cultural values of cities can be managed, archived, and explored at any scale (Gabellone, 2022; Massafra et al., 2022; Niccolucci et al., 2022);
8. Health and medical services. People who have difficulties accessing natural environments can benefit from restorative natural environments using digital twins, which can combine spatial data, such as topography, high-resolution aerial images, and building and vegetation models. By enriching models with sound and time- and physics-based changes, such as weather conditions, natural environments can be accessed virtually to some degree (Ferdousi et al., 2021; Hejtmánek et al., 2022; Kobayashi et al., 2022; Spitzer et al., 2023; Zhou et al., 2022);
9. Land administration systems. Countries worldwide have started realising the power of digital twins in delineating ownership boundaries in the third dimension of space. Digital twins can better contextualise rights, restrictions, and responsibilities both above and underground. It is much easier to communicate who owns what using digital twins, making it clear as to what owners or occupiers can or cannot do about what they own and what they are accountable for in communal spaces;
10. Asset management is an essential application of digital twins. Three-dimensional representations of assets in a geographical context are the first step in using digital twins to record and account for assets. By building virtual models and using augmented reality, virtual reality, and mixed reality systems, one can improve the planning, inspection, repair, and replacement of assets more efficiently than using traditional 2D asset management approaches (Abdelmoti et al., 2021; Arisekola & Madson, 2023; Chen et al., 2021; Macchi et al., 2018; Saback et al., 2022);
11. Public safety. Digital twins can help public safety on several fronts, such as mapping public spaces in 3D, running training sessions, improving preparedness for incidents and emergency situations, routing for first responder and evacuation simulation, and situational awareness;
12. Tourism. Tourist destinations can leverage digital twins to provide interactive and immersive experiences. Virtual replicas of destinations can be used to showcase attractions, accommodation, and activities,

allowing tourists to explore and plan their visit in advance (Baker et al., 2023; Litavniece et al., 2023; Ssin et al., 2021).

13. Construction engineering. Digital twins have a wide range of applications in construction engineering, covering the entire life cycle of buildings and infrastructure. Digital twins can be used in planning, design, construction, operation, and demolition (Hu et al., 2022; Opoku et al., 2021, 2022; Rafsanjani & Nabizadeh, 2023; Zhang et al., 2022).

1.6 Summary

In this chapter, we made a case for the use of digital twins in different aspects of cities. We noted that cities worldwide will continue to accommodate more people than rural areas. We also noted that cities are an import development engine for countries worldwide. As such, we argued that the planning, developing, and managing of cities requires the appropriate tools, one of which is digital twins. We positioned digital twins within a broader smart city framework and explained their relation to other smart city components. We then outlined a series of applications of digital twins. In the next chapters, we take a look at the geospatial aspect of digital twins, including GIS and BIM, starting by exploring the data models that underpin digital twins.

Bibliography

Abdelmoti, A. M., Shafiq, M. T., & Ur Rehman, M. S. (2021). Applications of digital twins for asset management in AEC/FM industry – A literature review. *Proceedings of the 8th Zero Energy Mass Custom Home (ZEMCH) 2021 International Conference*, 26–28 October 2021, Dubai, UAE, pp. 408–415. www.zemch.org/proceedings/2021/ZEMCH2021.pdf.

Alves, S. F. R., Uribe-Quevedo, A., Chen, D., Morris, J., & Radmard, S. (2022). Developing a VR simulator for robotics navigation and human robot interactions employing digital twins. *2022 IEEE Conference on Virtual Reality and 3D User Interfaces Abstracts and Workshops, VRW*, Christchurch, New Zealand, 2022, pp. 121–125. https://doi.org/10.1109/VRW55335.2022.00036

Arisekola, K., & Madson, K. (2023). Digital twins for asset management: Social network analysis-based review. *Automation in Construction, 150.* https://doi.org/10.1016/j.autcon.2023.104833

Baker, D., Botev, N., Garbett, A., Gietel-Basten, S., Luchsinger, G., Nandagiri, R., & others. (2023). *State of World Population Report 2023*. New York: UNFPA.

Baker, J., Nam, K., & Dutt, C. S. (2023). A user experience perspective on heritage tourism in the metaverse: Empirical evidence and design dilemmas for VR. *Information Technology and Tourism, 25*(3). https://doi.org/10.1007/s40558-023-00256-x

Banaeian Far, S., & Imani Rad, A. (2022). Applying digital twins in Metaverse: User interface, security and privacy challenges. *Journal of Metaverse, 2*(1).

Barresi, A. (2023). Urban digital twin and urban planning for sustainable cities. *TECHNE, 25*. https://doi.org/10.36253/techne-13568

Beheshti, M., Naeimi, T., Hudson, T. E., Feng, C., Mongkolwat, P., Riewpaiboon, W., Seiple, W., Vedanthan, R., & Rizzo, J. R. (2023). A smart service system for spatial intelligence and onboard navigation for individuals with Visual Impairment (VIS4ION Thailand): Study protocol of a randomized controlled trial of visually impaired students at the Ratchasuda College, Thailand. *Trials, 24*(1). https://doi.org/10.1186/s13063-023-07173-8

Bertinelli, L., & Black, D. (2004). Urbanization and growth. *Journal of Urban Economics, 56*(1). https://doi.org/10.1016/j.jue.2004.03.003

Bettencourt, L. M. A., Lobo, J., Helbing, D., Kühnert, C., & West, G. B. (2007). Growth, innovation, scaling, and the pace of life in cities. *Proceedings of the National Academy of Sciences of the United States of America, 104*(17). https://doi.org/10.1073/pnas.0610172104

Chen, L., Xie, X., Lu, Q., Parlikad, A. K., Pitt, M., & Yang, J. (2021). Gemini principles-based digital twin maturity model for asset management. *Sustainability (Switzerland), 13*(15). https://doi.org/10.3390/su13158224

Cocchia, A. (2014). *Smart and Digital City: A Systematic Literature Review*. https://doi.org/10.1007/978-3-319-06160-3_2

Colenbrander, S. (2016, October). Cities as engines of economic growth: The case for providing basic infrastructure and services in urban areas. International Institute for Environment and Development. www.iied.org/10801iied

Dembski, F., Yamu, C. & Ssner, U. W.. (2019). Digital twin, virtual reality and space syntax: Civic engagement and decision support for smart, sustainable cities. *Proceedings of the 12th International Space Syntax Symposium*, Beijing, pp. 316.1–316.13.

Ferdousi, R., Hossain, M. A., & El Saddik, A. (2021). IoT-enabled model for Digital Twin of Mental Stress (DTMS). *2021 IEEE Globecom Workshops, GC Wkshps 2021 – Proceedings*. https://doi.org/10.1109/GCWkshps52748.2021.9681996

Ferré-Bigorra, J., Casals, M., & Gangolells, M. (2022). The adoption of urban digital twins. *Cities, 131*. https://doi.org/10.1016/j.cities.2022.103905

Gabellone, F. (2022). Digital twin: A new perspective for cultural heritage management and fruition. *Acta IMEKO, 11*(1). https://doi.org/10.21014/acta_imeko.v11i1.1085

Hejtmánek, L., Hůla, M., Herrová, A., & Surový, P. (2022). Forest digital twin as a relaxation environment: A pilot study. *Frontiers in Virtual Reality, 3*. https://doi.org/10.3389/frvir.2022.1033708

Hu, W., Lim, K. Y. H., & Cai, Y. (2022). Digital twin and Industry 4.0 enablers in building and construction: A survey. *Buildings, 12*(11). https://doi.org/10.3390/buildings12112004

Jagatheesaperumal, S. K., Yang, Z., Yang, Q., Huang, C., Xu, W., Shikh-Bahaei, M., & Zhang, Z. (2023). Semantic-aware digital twin for Metaverse: A comprehensive review. *IEEE Wireless Communications, 30*(4). https://doi.org/10.1109/MWC.003.2200616

Khor, N., Arimah, B., Otieno, R. O., van Oostrum, M., Mutinda, M., & Martins, J. O. (2022). *World cities report 2022: Envisaging the future of cities*. UN-Habitat, Nairobi, Kenya.

Kismul, A., Al-Khateeb, H., & Jahankhani, H. (2023). A critical review of digital twin confidentiality in a smart city. In *Advanced Sciences and Technologies for Security Applications*. https://doi.org/10.1007/978-3-031-20160-8_25

Ko, M., & Lee, S. (2022). Exploring the knowledge structure of digital twin & Metaverse. *Journal of Korea Technology Innovation Society, 25*(6). https://doi.org/10.35978/jktis.2022.12.25.6.1185

Kobayashi, T., Fukae, K., Imai, T., & Arai, K. (2022). Digital twin agent for super-aged society. *Digest of Technical Papers – IEEE International Conference on Consumer Electronics, 2022-January*. https://doi.org/10.1109/ICCE53296.2022.9730230

Litavniece, L., Kodors, S., Adamoniene, R., & Kijasko, J. (2023). Digital twin: An approach to enhancing tourism competitiveness. *Worldwide Hospitality and Tourism Themes, 15*(5). https://doi.org/10.1108/WHATT-06-2023-0074

Lv, Z., Xie, S., Li, Y., Shamim Hossain, M., & El Saddik, A. (2022). Building the Metaverse by digital twins at all scales, state, relation. *Virtual Reality and Intelligent Hardware, 4*(6). https://doi.org/10.1016/j.vrih.2022.06.005

Macchi, M., Roda, I., Negri, E., & Fumagalli, L. (2018). Exploring the role of digital twin for asset lifecycle management. *IFAC-Papers OnLine, 51*(11). https://doi.org/10.1016/j.ifacol.2018.08.415

Massafra, A., Predari, G., & Gulli, R. (2022). Towards digital twins driven cultural heritage management: A HBIM-based workflow for energy improvement of modern buildings. *International Archives of the Photogrammetry, Remote Sensing and Spatial Information Sciences – ISPRS Archives, 46*(5/W1-2022). https://doi.org/10.5194/isprs-archives-XLVI-5-W1-2022-149-2022

Mourtzis, D. (2023). Digital twin inception in the Era of industrial metaverse. *Frontiers in Manufacturing Technology, 3*. https://doi.org/10.3389/fmtec.2023.1155735

Musse, J., Rosenzweig, J. D., Ahmad, K., Imtiaz Jabeen, N., & Winther, S. H. (2019). *Ethics of personal data in IoT*. Roskilde University. https://rucforsk.ruc.dk/ws/portalfiles/portal/66460974/Ethics_of_Personal_Data_in_IoT.pdf

Niccolucci, F., Felicetti, A., & Hermon, S. (2022). Populating the data space for cultural heritage with heritage digital twins. *Data, 7*(8). https://doi.org/10.3390/data7080105

Opoku, D. G. J., Perera, S., Osei-Kyei, R., & Rashidi, M. (2021). Digital twin application in the construction industry: A literature review. *Journal of Building Engineering, 40*. https://doi.org/10.1016/j.jobe.2021.102726

Opoku, D. G. J., Perera, S., Osei-Kyei, R., Rashidi, M., Famakinwa, T., & Bamdad, K. (2022). Drivers for digital twin adoption in the construction industry: A systematic literature review. *Buildings, 12*(2). https://doi.org/10.3390/buildings12020113

Papagiannidis, S., Bourlakis, M., & Li, F. (2008). Making real money in virtual worlds: MMORPGs and emerging business opportunities, challenges and ethical implications in metaverses. *Technological Forecasting and Social Change, 75*(5). https://doi.org/10.1016/j.techfore.2007.04.007

Qi, Y., Li, H., Pang, Z., Gao, W., & Liu, C. (2022). A case study of the relationship between vegetation coverage and urban heat Island in a Coastal City by applying digital twins. *Frontiers in Plant Science, 13.* https://doi.org/10.3389/fpls.2022.861768

Rafsanjani, H. N., & Nabizadeh, A. H. (2023). Towards digital architecture, engineering, and construction (AEC) industry through virtual design and construction (VDC) and digital twin. *Energy and Built Environment, 4*(2). https://doi.org/10.1016/j.enbenv.2021.10.004

Ricciardi, G., & Callegari, G. (2023). Digital twins for climate-neutral and resilient cities. State of the art and future development as tools to support urban decision-making. In *Urban Book Series: Vol. Part F813.* https://doi.org/10.1007/978-3-031-29515-7_55

Saback, V., Popescu, C., Blanksvärd, T., & Täljsten, B. (2022). Asset management of existing concrete bridges using digital twins and BIM: A state-of-the-art literature review. *Nordic Concrete Research, 66*(1). https://doi.org/10.2478/ncr-2021-0020

Samanta, S., Sarkar, A., & Bulo, Y. (2022). Secure smart city infrastructure using digital twin and blockchain. *Lecture Notes in Networks and Systems, 392.* https://doi.org/10.1007/978-981-19-0619-0_33

Schrotter, G., & Hürzeler, C. (2020). The digital twin of the city of Zurich for urban planning. *PFG – Journal of Photogrammetry, Remote Sensing and Geoinformation Science, 88*(1). https://doi.org/10.1007/s41064-020-00092-2

Spitzer, M., Dattner, I., & Zilcha-Mano, S. (2023). Digital twins and the future of precision mental health. *Frontiers in Psychiatry, 14.* https://doi.org/10.3389/fpsyt.2023.1082598

Ssin, S., Suh, M., Lee, J., Jung, T., & Woo, W. (2021). Science tour and business model using digital twin-based augmented reality. In *Augmented Reality and Virtual Reality*, M. Claudia tom Dieck, Timothy H. Jung, & Sandra M. C. Loureiro (eds.), pp. 267–276. Springer. https://doi.org/10.1007/978-3-030-68086-2_20

Svelec, D., Bjelcic, N., & Blazekovic, M. (2020). Smart cities as an opportunity and challenge for people with disabilities. *2020 43rd International Convention on Information, Communication and Electronic Technology, MIPRO 2020 – Proceedings.* https://doi.org/10.23919/MIPRO48935.2020.9245183

Tacchino, A., Podda, J., Bergamaschi, V., Pedullà, L., & Brichetto, G. (2023). Cognitive rehabilitation in multiple sclerosis: Three digital ingredients to address current and future priorities. *Frontiers in Human Neuroscience, 17.* https://doi.org/10.3389/fnhum.2023.1130231

Tang, Y., Gao, F., Wang, C., Huang, M. M., Wu, M., Li, H., & Li, Z. (2023). Vertical Greenery System (VGS) renovation for sustainable Arcade-housing: Building energy efficiency analysis based on digital twin. *Sustainability (Switzerland), 15*(3). https://doi.org/10.3390/su15032310

UN-Habitat (2011). *The economic role of cities.* United Nations Human Settlements Programme.

Vildjiounaite, E., Kallio, J., Kantorovitch, J., Kinnula, A., Ferreira, S., Rodrigues, M. A., & Rocha, N. (2023). Challenges of learning human digital twin: Case study of mental wellbeing: Using sensor data and machine learning to create HDT. *ACM International Conference Proceeding Series.* https://doi.org/10.1145/3594806.3596538

Zhang, J., Cheng, J. C. P., Chen, W., & Chen, K. (2022). Digital twins for construction sites: Concepts, LoD definition, and applications. *Journal of Management in Engineering, 38*(2). https://doi.org/10.1061/(asce)me.1943-5479.0000948

Zhou, H., Gao, J. Y., & Chen, Y. (2022). The paradigm and future value of the metaverse for the intervention of cognitive decline. *Frontiers in Public Health 10*. https://doi.org/10.3389/fpubh.2022.1016680

Zygiaris, S. (2013). Smart city reference model: Assisting planners to conceptualize the building of smart city innovation ecosystems. *Journal of the Knowledge Economy*, 4(2). https://doi.org/10.1007/s13132-012-0089-4

2

Fundamentals of 3D Modelling

2.1 Introduction

Humans see the world in 3D. People cannot comprehend natural or built environments without the third dimension of height. Different professions, such as land surveyors, geographers, and artists, represent and abstract what they see based on the context of their work. The absolute and relative positions of objects, the scale and level details that are required in their application, and the proximity and relation between objects and surrounding objects all influence their representation.

Abstracting the world and representing objects have long been done in 2D. From engraving stones to drawing on paper and digital representations of natural and built environments, the fundamentals of representation have remained the same: Abstract the world using points, lines, and polygons and scale objects proportionally and position them in space such that the proximities between them are representative of the real world.

Before the computer age and the availability of digital storage and processing, attempts to use 3D spaces to represent the features of the world were also practised (Figure 2.1 and Figure 2.2). While the utility and practicality of these representations have been limited, the fundamentals of 2D representation have extended to using volumes and surfaces in addition to points, lines, and polygons to represent the third dimension.

In the next section, we review how objects of the world can be abstracted in 3D in terms of geometrical and mathematical constructs.

2.2 Abstracting the World in 3D

2.2.1 Using Points

Objects can be represented using collections of points in 3D spaces. Points in these representations should have 3D coordinates. Objects in 3D can be represented using collections of points that have latitude, longitude, and

DOI: 10.1201/9781351200950-2

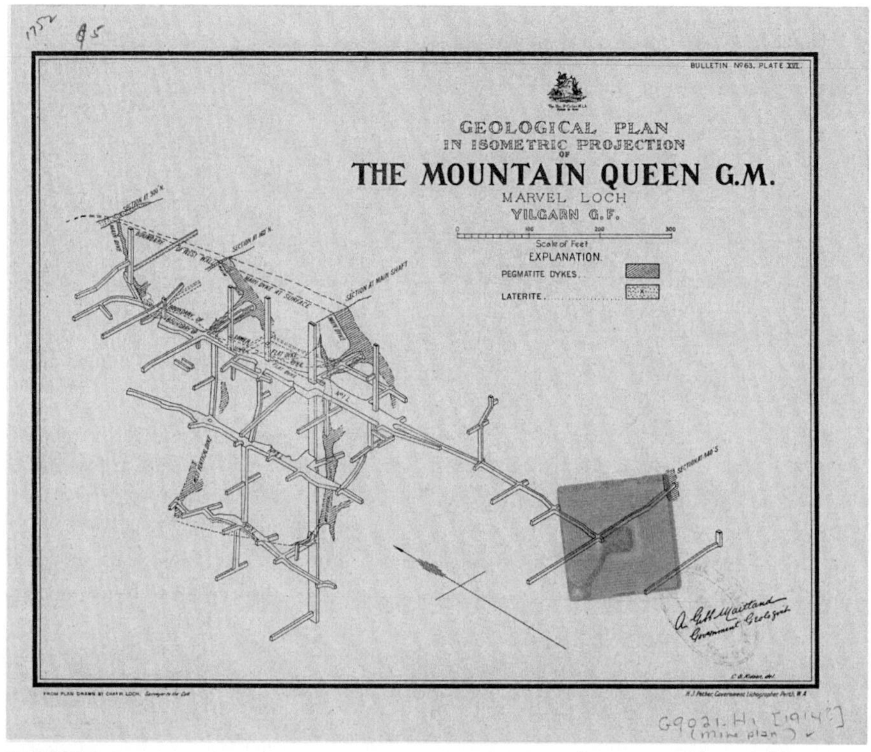

FIGURE 2.1
Geological plan in an isometric projection of the Mountain Queen G.M. (Geological Survey of Western Australia & Loch, 1914.)

height coordinates in a geographical coordinate system or an arbitrary cartesian coordinate system using x, y, and z axes.

Point clouds, which are generated using different approaches, such as laser scanning or photogrammetric methods, are examples of point-based object representation. This representation method is used to record the surfaces of natural and built environments. For example, point clouds are used to represent urban environments, including buildings, trees, and terrain (Figure 2.3).

There are a number of data formats that support the point-based data model, such as LAS, LAZ(LASzip), e57, and PTS.

LAS is an Open Geospatial Consortium community standard, developed and owned by the American Society for Photogrammetry and Remote Sensing (ASPRS). It facilitates interoperability between different software tools. LAZ is the compressed format of LAS, which is generated using an open-source tool called LASzip. E57 is another standard for point-cloud data,

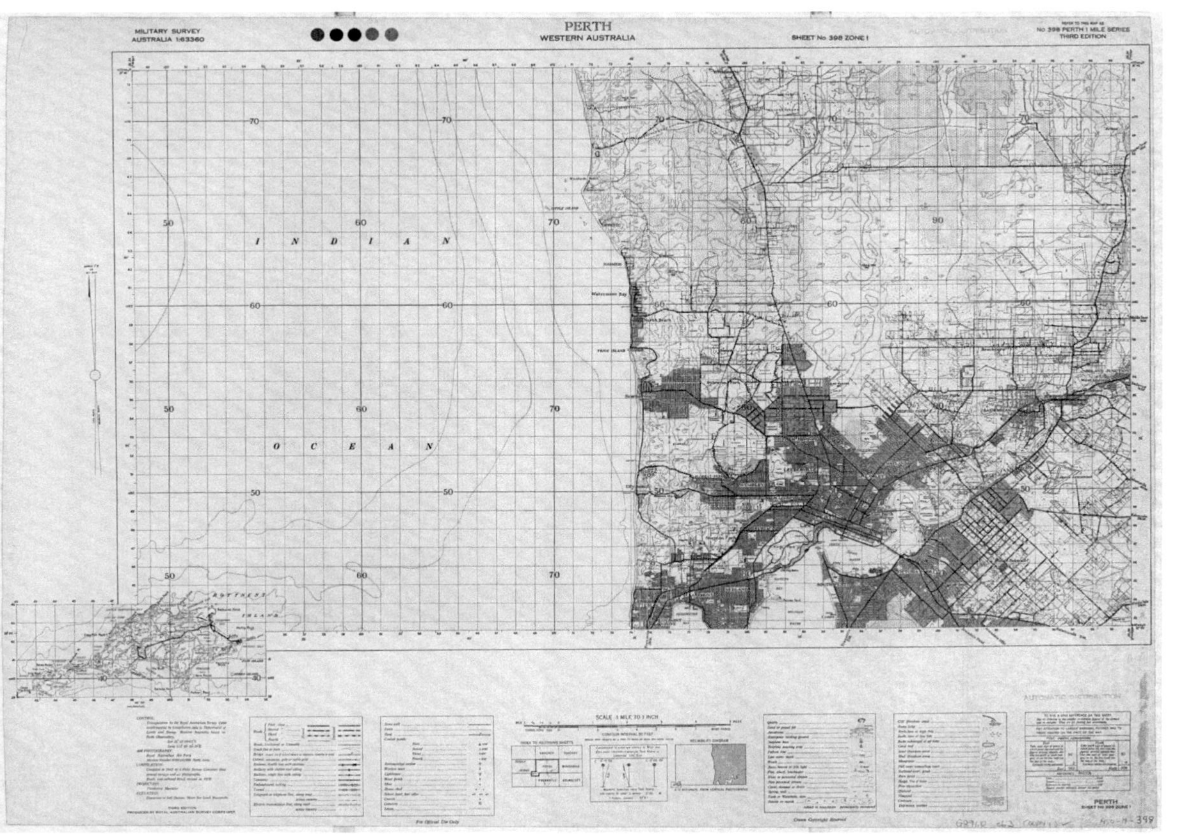

FIGURE 2.2
Use of contour lines to depict the third dimension of land and sea. (Australian Army, Royal Australian Survey Corps. et al., 1957.)

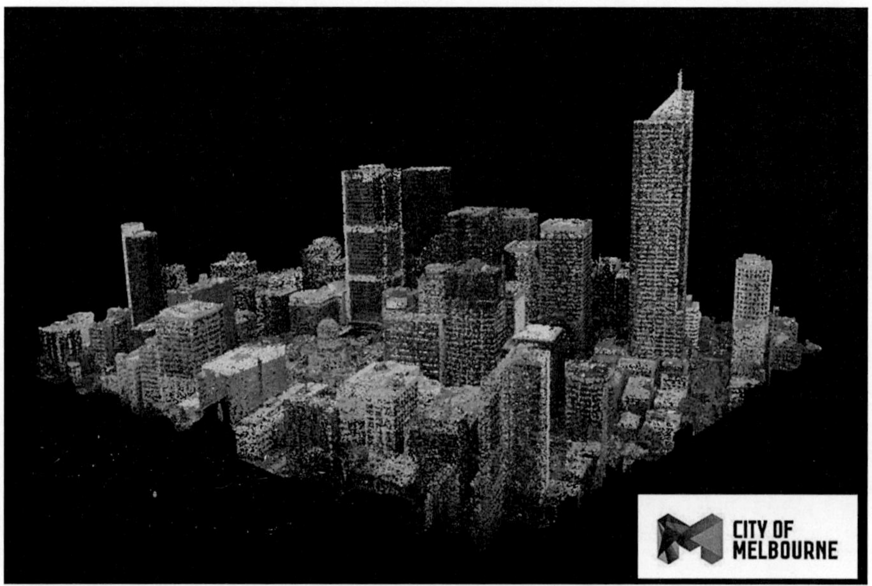

FIGURE 2.3
Point-based representation of the City of Melbourne, Australia. (City of Melbourne Open Data Team, 2018.)

developed by ASTM International. The LAS format was driven by aerial mapping requirements, while e57 was developed for general purposes.

A PTS file is a file in text format that is used for storing point-based data. The initial line indicates the total number of points in the file. Subsequent lines contain seven values each: The first three represent the (x, y, z) coordinates of the points; the fourth denotes an "intensity" value; and the last three indicate the (R, G, B) colour estimates. Intensity refers to the strength or amplitude of a reflected laser pulse from a surface. The intensity value provides information about the reflectivity or brightness of a surface at a particular point on the Earth's surface, where 0 indicates a very poor return and 255 signifies a very strong return.

Sample PTS files include the following:

```
741523
-0.11025 -2.1806 8.10981 54 53 44 65
-0.62016 -1.94527 6.49447 227 224 230 225
-0.4366 -2.24446 7.81288 61 56 56 68
-0.42017 -1.61698 7.71458 63 58 50 71
-0.656 -2.36051 7.45187 151 140 167 161
-0.62371 -1.63502 7.56876 167 163 175 175
-0.72829 -2.37286 6.44905 209 204 217 211
-0.67614 -2.58739 7.46484 152 144 155 156
```

2.2.2 Using Planar Surfaces

In this representation method, real-world objects are abstracted using the intersections of planar surfaces. In this context, we define a surface as a two-dimensional manifold in a three-dimensional Euclidian space. The intersections create an array of polygons with shared sides and vertices. In this context, a polygon consists of several cyclically ordered vertices and an equal number of sides that consecutively join the vertices (Figure 2.4). The last side joins the first and last vertices and no three successive points are colinear.

The simplest form of polygons for abstracting objects is the triangle. Triangular irregular networks (TINs) (De Berg et al., 2008) are one of the methods that are widely used in various applications in GIS. This approach is a pragmatic method for modelling the surface shapes of objects for which it is practical to measure height for every point, such as terrain (Figure 2.5).

Another approach that utilises the planar surface principle is boundary representation, or B-Rep (Zhu et al., 2020). The total surfaces of objects in 3D spaces are broken into surface boundaries. Each surface boundary is a polygon that shares edges and vertices with other surface boundaries (Figure 2.6). This approach is widely used to model built environments, such as buildings and infrastructure, where objects can be depicted in 3D.

2.2.3 Using Primitive Solids

In contrast to surface geometry, we can use solid geometry (Zhu et al., 2020) to abstract the complexities of 3D spaces. Solid are volumes in 3D Euclidian spaces that are bound by surfaces. There are simple solid geometries that can be used to construct more complex shapes, which are called primitive solids. Primitive solids include spheres, cubes, cones, and cylinders. Using the set theory, we can construct complex geometries by utilising unions, intersections, and subtraction operations (Figure 2.7). This method is called constructive solid geometry.

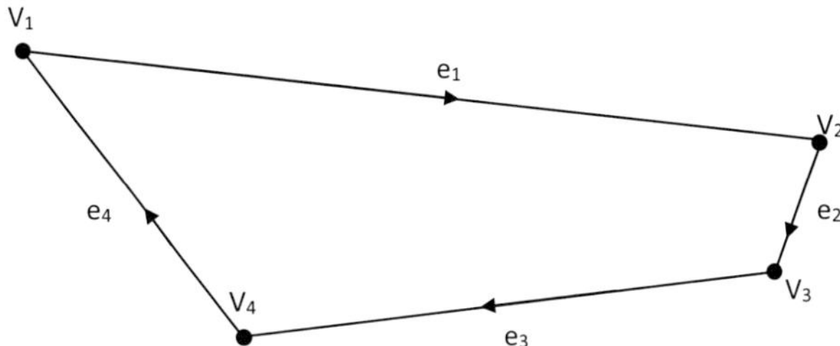

FIGURE 2.4
Cyclically ordered vertices in a planar surface, which is suitable for use as a building block for 3D data representation.

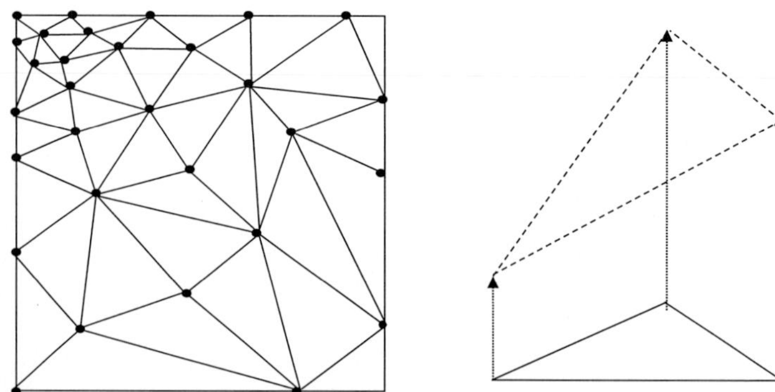

FIGURE 2.5
Planar (left) and isometric (right) views of TIN, which can be used to represent the third dimension.

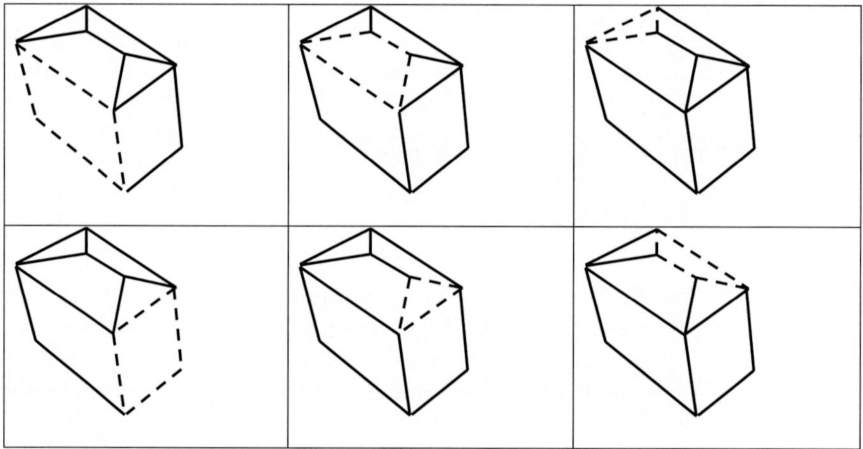

FIGURE 2.6
Representing an object using its surface boundaries.

2.2.4 Using an Array of Volumes

Another way to represent spaces is to break them into 3D arrays of volumes. In this approach, the entire spaces, whether any objects occupy any particular parts of the spaces or not, are covered by volumes (Figure 2.8). Each volume is assigned a value representing the feature in that space. If the volumes are isotropic (cube) and identical in dimension (Figure 2.1), they are often called voxels (Aleksandrov et al., 2021). Voxels are similar to pixels, which are the regular 2D grids used in image-based methods.

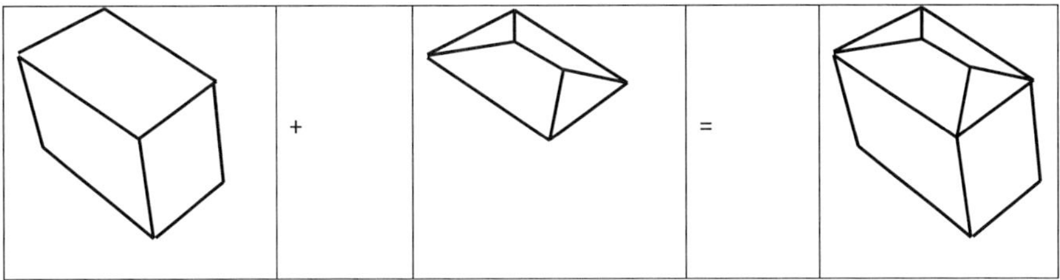

FIGURE 2.7
Constructive solid geometry.

FIGURE 2.8
Voxel representation of an object (note that the shaded areas that are not occupied by the object are also voxelised (generated by artificial intelligence)).

2.3 3D Data Models

While at the conceptual level, it is easy to represent or design spaces and the objects within them using the above concepts; however, the diversity of objects and their relationships in the context of space make it difficult to use the above approaches without formalising them in data models. As such, numerous data models have been developed in various file formats to model the world on computers. These data models were developed from two broad perspectives: Representing existing objects within given spaces or creating representations of objects that do not yet exist. While the latter resides in the realm of designing new environments, the former focuses on mapping existing environments. Either way, data modelling follows a similar approach by understanding the requirements of the application disciplines in which the data are used.

The design discipline is driven by practical and regulatory frameworks that facilitate the creation and improvement of cities, buildings, transport networks, bridges, landscapes, environment, city furniture, etc. The design realm innovates schemes to enhance the way people live in and interact with built environments. As such, data models designed for this discipline provide more flexibility to allow for creativity and facilitate the physical delivery and realisation of each design.

IFC is a standard data model that is widely used in the design discipline (Borrmann et al., 2018). IFC stands for Industry Foundation Classes, and it is an open standard file format that is used in the architecture, engineering, and construction (AEC) industry for the exchange and sharing of digital information about building and construction projects. IFC is maintained by building SMART International, a non-profit organisation that is dedicated to developing open standards for built environments. We will introduce IFC fully in other chapters of this book. We note that IFC primarily uses constructive solid geometry to model objects.

The mapping discipline is driven by the level of detail that is needed in its application domains, such as land administration, urban planning and design, disaster and emergency management, asset management, and many more. Significant factors in the mapping discipline include how environments are abstracted by measuring what is needed for specific applications, how collected data can best be recorded, and how the data can best be analysed and visualised to meet the needs of the application domain. As such, the data models used in the mapping discipline are more focused on classifying built-environment objects into groups that share similar properties to make the recording, retrieval, and analysis of data more efficient.

A standard data model that is widely used in the mapping discipline is CityGML (City Geography Markup Language), which is an open international standard data model for the representation and exchange of 3D city models and urban information, developed by the Open Geospatial Consortium (OGC). It is designed to support the storage, exchange, and sharing of digital 3D models of urban environments and city structures. CityGML allows for the detailed representation of the 3D geometry and semantics of urban structures, including buildings, roads, bridges, vegetation, and other city features. As such, it is essential to understand the context in which a data format is used.

2.4 3D Spatial Database Systems

Database systems are computerised filing systems that allow for new data to be added to systems and the records within systems to be inserted, retrieved, changed, or deleted. Spatial databases are a subset of database systems that are specifically designed to handle spatial data. We note that 3D spatial data can also be stored in file-based systems. Prominent examples of file-based data storage were introduced earlier in this chapter, including LAS, e57, PTS, IFC, and CityGML. In this section, we focus on database systems and how they are managed.

2.4.1 Recording and Accessing 3D Point Representation

3D points offer the most straightforward representations of built environments. Objects are abstracted using points with 3D coordinates in specific coordinate systems. The points are given unique identification number (IDs) and the associated coordinates are stored in databases.

The main issue with point-based representations of urban environments is the size of the data. The more granular the point-based representation, the larger the amount of data. Large amounts of data make retrieving and analysing data difficult. Ideally, when the proximities of points in the real world are preserved in the storage of the data, the data can be retrieved and analysed more efficiently. It is important to note that computer memory is one-dimensional and the efficient storage of three-dimensional data, such as point clouds, is a significant challenge.

Space-filling curves offer an approach for mapping from higher dimensional spaces to one-dimensional spaces. The benefits of utilising space-filling curves to index multidimensional data were explored in Lawder and King (2000). Numerous space-filling curves have been developed, preserving varying degrees of proximity in data. A comprehensive overview of space-filling curves, such as Z-order and Hilbert, is available (van Oosterom, 1999).

2.4.2 Planar Surfaces

There are several options for representing objects using planar surfaces. While points are the basic building blocks of planar surfaces, constructing planar surfaces can be done in several ways, depending on the atomic surface geometry.

There are three broad approaches for storing TINs, which are based on vertices, edges, and triangles. In the vertex-based approach, vertices are stored using their coordinates, as well as all of the adjacent vertices that are determined by the edges that connect them and the maximum number of adjacent vertices (Figure 2.9).

ID	x	y	z	Edges	Maximum Number
V_1	0	0	0	e_1, e_2, e_3	3

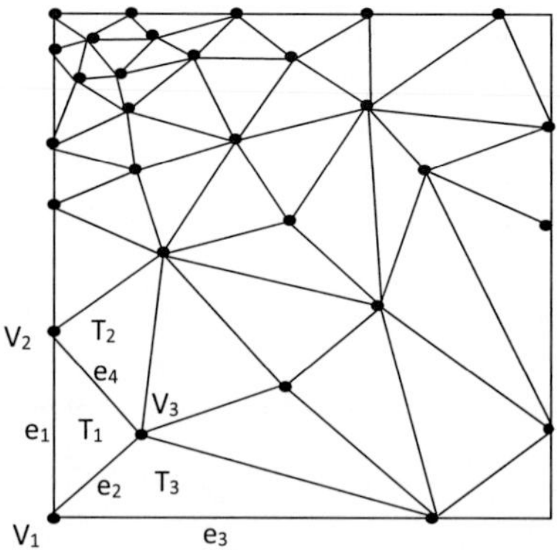

FIGURE 2.9
Storing a TIN model.

Alternatively, adjacent vertices can be stored in separate records and each vertex has its own record.

ID	x	y	z
V_1	0	0	0

ID	Edges	Maximum Number
V1	e_1, e_2, e_3	3

In the triangle-based approach, triangles are stored together with the coordinates of their vertices and the reference numbers for neighbouring triangles. An alternative to this approach is to store vertices separately and only refer to them as part of the triangle records.

ID	V_a	V_b	V_c	T_a	T_b	T_c
T_1	V_1	V_2	V_3	T_2	T_3	

In the edge-based approach, vertices are stored in separate tables, while edges are stored using start and end vertices and left and right triangles. Then, two tables for triangles are created: One table is for the three vertices of the triangles and the other table is for the edges of the triangles.

ID	**Start**	**End**	T_R	T_L
e_1	V_1	V_2	T_1	
e_4	V_2	V_3	T_2	T_1
e_2	V_3	V_1	T_3	T_1

ID	V_a	V_b	V_c
T_1	V_1	V_2	V_3

ID	e_a	e_b	e_c
T_1	e_1	e_4	e_2

B-Rep has been manifested in various database systems in different ways, but the fundamentals of storage are very similar. Every 3D object is a composition of several surfaces that represent the outer surface of the object, which is often called the outer shell. Each shell is formed using lines that represent the perimeter of the shell, which are often referred to as edges. Similarly, each edge is represented using its start and end points, which are called vertices or nodes (Figure 2.10). The concept of rings is used to represent holes in surfaces.

ID	**x**	**y**	**z**
V_1	2	0	2
V_2	2	0	4
V_3	4	0	4
V_4	4	0	2
V_5	2	2	2
V_6	2	2	4
V_7	4	2	4
V_8	4	2	2

ID	**Min Corner**	**Max Corner**
P_1	V_1	V_8
P_2	V_2	V_7
P_3	V_4	V_7
P_4	V_1	V_6
P_5	V_1	V_3
P_6	V_5	V_7

ID	**Polygons**
C_1	$P_{1,}$ $P_{2,}$ $P_{3,}$ $P_{4,}$ $P_{5,}$ P_6

2.4.3 Constructive Solid Geometry

The problem with storing 3D data using solid geometries can be formulated into two stages. The first stage is the storage of primitive solids that are used

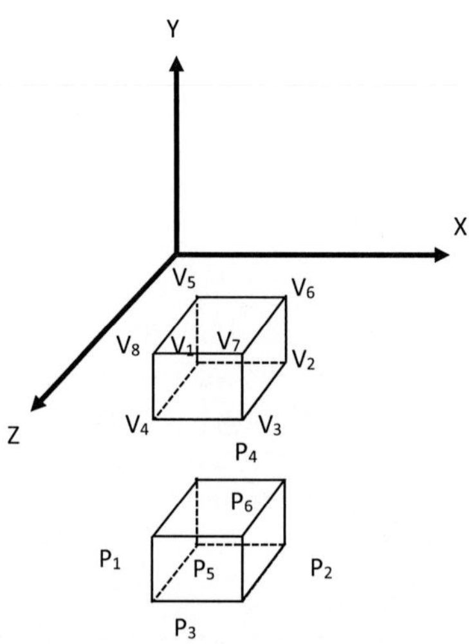

FIGURE 2.10
B-rep storage using polygons and vertices.

to create composite solids. The second stage is storing combinations that are regulated by the Boolean set theory.

To store primitive solid objects, we need to store their positions in relation to the coordinate system and the values of the dimension parameters. For example, the location of cubes in a database are stored in one table, while their dimensions are stored in a separate table. An alternative method for storing cubes as solid objects in databases is to use the minimum and maximum coordinate values of the cubes, reducing the number of tables in relational databases. For instance, the above cube is simply stored using its minimum and maximum coordinates, as follows:

ID	x	y	z
V_1	2	0	2
V_7	4	2	4

ID	Minimum Vertex	Maximum Vertex
C_1	V_1	V_7

2.4.4 Storing an Array of Volumes

To store arrays of volumes in databases, it is critical to understand how the elements of the arrays are positioned and what characteristics they possess.

While the latter is an attribution issue, the former is an inherently spatial and proximity matter.

Octree is recognised as an efficient method for storing the proximities of arrays. In the Octree approach, spaces are enclosed using cubes and each cube is subdivided into eight subcubes. This subdivision recursively continues until the point at which the desired atomic size of a volume is reached.

From a database perspective, what needs to be established is the relation between the voxels that are contained by the Octree partitions. In other words, a table is required to store each component of Octree, called leaves, using a unique ID. A table is also required to store leaves' attributions and their location in the Octree using the unique ID of the Octree. Each leaf voxel, i.e., the finest desired space partition, is stored and a reference is given to its parent. A basic Octree algorithm is provided in the following section.

2.5 Visualising 3D Objects

The 3D visualisation of objects or scenes is a function of four factors: The point of view or where one wants to look at the object from; the amount of data that is supposed to be viewed by the viewer; what details are required or can be seen by the viewer; finally, how close the viewer wants the visualisation to be to the reality of the object. In a more methodical approach, we can view 3D visualisation as a four-step process that defines the viewpoint, view volume, and visible surfaces of an object and then finally renders the object.

To be able to implement the process, we need to define where the object is located and where the viewpoint is. To do this, we define two spaces: The object space and the view space. The object space is a cartesian space that provides us with the object's location (Figure 2.11).

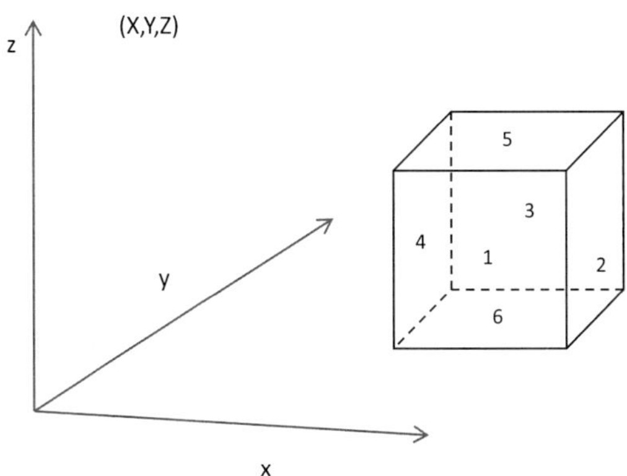

FIGURE 2.11
The object space where an object is localised.

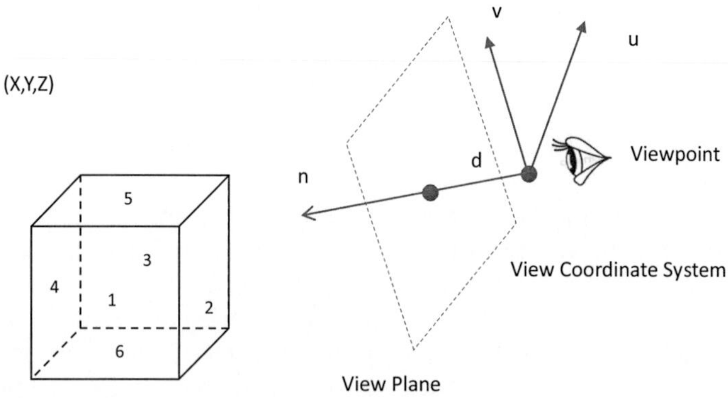

FIGURE 2.12
View space, which includes a viewpoint, view coordinate system, and view plane. (Adopted from Hughes, J. F. et al., 2013.)

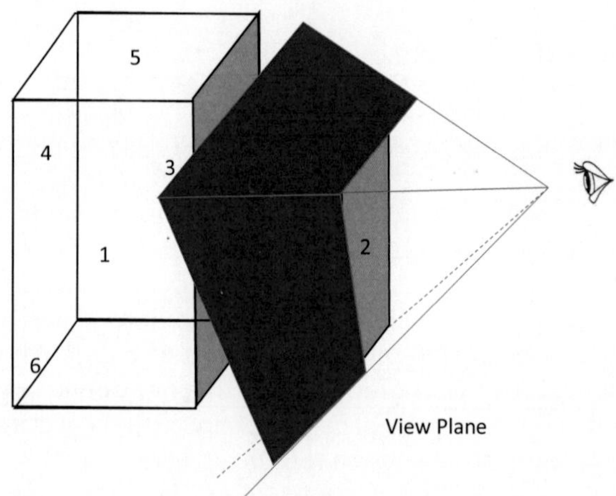

FIGURE 2.13
View volume, which is determined by a view plane.

Similarly, the view space is a 3D cartesian space that is defined by the location viewpoint and the direction from which the object is seen (Figure 2.12).

In addition, we need to define a view plane, which helps to define the view volume, i.e., the amount of data required to be seen from the object (Figure 2.13).

Through transformation between spaces, we can relate these two spaces such that when you change the viewpoint and view direction, the object visualisation changes.

Therefore, we can change the viewpoint and see different parts of objects in natural visibility. We can also specify what we want to be visible in scenes, apart from the natural visibility. We can specify whether certain objects in scenes or certain surfaces of objects are visualised or not (Figure 2.14).

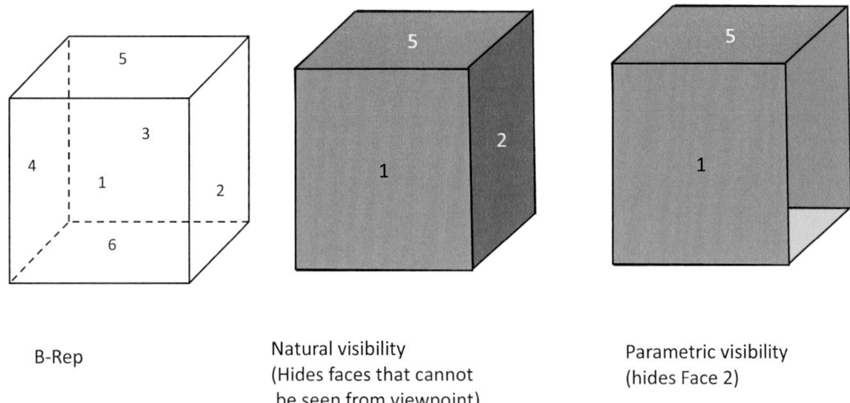

FIGURE 2.14
How a 3D object based on B-Rep is naturally and parametrically visualised.

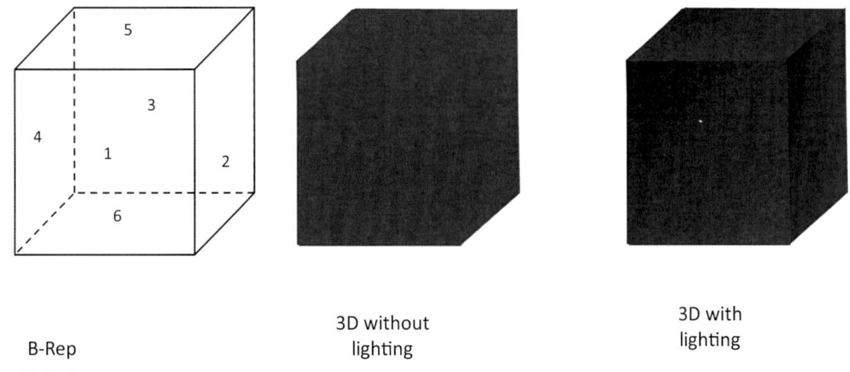

FIGURE 2.15
Lighting effect in a visualisation of a B-Rep object.

The final step in visualisation is rendering. Rendering includes applying lighting effects on scenes or objects to provide a 3D impression. When we visualise objects on computers, smartphones, or tablet screens, they are 2D; therefore, unless we apply lighting effects, we cannot imagine them in 3D (Figure 2.15).

2.6 Summary

This chapter discussed different theoretical approaches to abstracting the world in 3D. We also introduced some important data models that implement these theories. We noted that the theories can be implemented in various ways. As such, there are various data models with different utilities. We also explored how 3D data can be stored in database systems. We then introduced 3D visualisation theory and how different variables are important in visualisation. In the next chapter, we will introduce the fundamentals of BIM and build on what was introduced in this chapter.

Bibliography

Aleksandrov, M., Zlatanova, S., & Heslop, D. J. (2021). Voxelisation algorithms and data structures: A review. *Sensors, 21*(24). https://doi.org/10.3390/s21248241

Australia Army. Royal Australian Survey Corps., Australia Royal Australian Air Force, photographer, Australia. Army. Field Survey Company, 4th, compiler, & Western Australia. Department of Lands and Surveys. (1957). *Perth, Western Australia.* www.nla.gov.au/nla.obj-316497182

Borrmann, A., König, M., Koch, C., & Beetz, J. (2018). Building information modeling: Technology foundations and industry practice. In *Building Information Modeling: Technology Foundations and Industry Practice.* https://doi.org/10.1007/978-3-319-92862-3

City of Melbourne Open Data Team. (2018). City of Melbourne 3D Point Cloud *2018* [Data set]. City of Melbourne. https://data.melbourne.vic.gov.au/explore/dataset/city-of-melbourne-3d-point-cloud-2018/information/.

De Berg, M., Cheong, O., Van Kreveld, M., & Overmars, M. (2008). Computational geometry: Algorithms and applications. *Computational Geometry: Algorithms and Applications.* https://doi.org/10.1007/978-3-540-77974-2

Geological Survey of Western Australia, & Loch, Chas. W. (1914). *Geological plan in isometric projection of the Mountain Queen G.M. Marvel Loch, Yilgarn G.F.* www.nla.gov.au/nla.obj-1509106843/view

Hughes, J. F., et al. (2013). *Computer Graphics: Principles and Practice* (3rd ed.). Upper Saddle River, NJ: Addison-Wesley Professional. ISBN: 978-321-39952-6.

Lawder, Jonathan K. and Peter J. H. King. (2000). "Using Space-Filling Curves for Multi-dimensional Indexing." British National Conference on Databases.

van Oosterom, P. (1999). Spatial access methods in geographical information systems principles, technical issues, management issues, and applications, edited by Longley, P.A., Goodchild, M.F., Maguire, D.J., & Rhind, D.W., *Geographical Information Systems: Principles, Techniques, Management and Applications. Volume 2: Management Issues and Applications* (xciii ed.). New York: Wiley, 385–400.

Zhu, J., Wu, P., Chen, M., Kim, M. J., Wang, X., & Fang, T. (2020). Automatically processing IFC clipping representation for BIM and GIS integration at the process level. *Applied Sciences (Switzerland), 10*(6). https://doi.org/10.3390/app10062009

3

Building Information Modelling

3.1 Introduction

BIM stands for building information modelling (a process) or a building information model (information). BIM, as a model, refers to digital representations of buildings or infrastructure assets, including their physical and functional characteristics. As a model, it allows stakeholders of construction projects, such as architects, engineers, contractors, and other professionals, to create, manage, and share detailed information about buildings or infrastructure projects throughout their life cycle, including their design, construction, operation, maintenance, and demolition (Azhar et al., 2012).

BIM enables stakeholders to create multidimensional models of buildings and infrastructure assets, which can be used for project management, cost estimation, the simulation of construction processes, the analysis of environmental impacts, and the detection of clashes or conflicts in the designs. BIM, as a process, can also manage and coordinate project data, such as schedules, cost estimates, and material quantities. BIM is increasingly becoming an essential tool in the construction industry, particularly with large projects, as it helps to improve efficiency, reduce costs, and enhance collaboration among project stakeholders (Eadie et al., 2013).

BIM can incorporate a wide range of details related to building or infrastructure assets, which are introduced in this section.

3.1.1 Geometry and Spatial Relationships

BIM, as information, comprises a 3D model, which represents the geometry of different elements of buildings or infrastructure assets. BIM also includes information about how the elements are spatially arranged in relation to each other.

This geometry may include different levels of detail, depending on the stage of the development of buildings or infrastructure assets. In the design stage, there are often fewer details included in BIM. Ideally, BIM should include all

DOI: 10.1201/9781351200950-3

of the information that is necessary to operate and maintain the buildings or infrastructure assets in the operation stage.

Level of Development (LoD) is often used to describe the detail and information that a BIM model contains (Latiffi et al., 2015). There is no standard for LoD, which can vary depending on the project, jurisdiction, or company involved in developing it. Generally, there are five LoDs in a BIM model, ranging from LoD 100 to LoD 500. LoD 100 is the lowest and often includes conceptual models with approximate geometries and generic data. LoD 200 includes models with more precise geometries for early cost estimation. LoD 300 includes detailed geometries and specific data about the building components and is used for the detailed scheduling of construction. LoD 400 includes precise geometries, specific data, and fabrication and assembly details and is suitable for fabrication and construction. LoD 500 includes models with precise geometries, specific data, and as-built information and is suitable for the management and maintenance of the assets.

3.1.2 Physical Properties

BIM, as information, can contain details about the physical properties of different building and infrastructure elements. This includes information about the materials used, weight, size, strength, thermal conductivity, and any other attribute involved in the life cycle of buildings and infrastructure assets. Essentially, BIM allows us to define and add properties to each and every element of buildings and infrastructure assets as needed and as is useful.

3.1.3 Time (4D) and Cost (5D) Information

BIM can include information related to the scheduling and sequencing of construction activities, as well as the time required to complete different tasks. This is often described as 4D in BIM, which facilitates the integration of scheduling data with a 3D model to create a virtual construction simulation that incorporates time (Boton et al., 2015). BIM can also include information related to the costs of different construction project elements, including materials, labour, and equipment. This is often described as 5D in BIM, which facilitates the integration of cost or budget data with a 3D model, as well as the project schedule. Therefore, 4D and 5D allow project managers and stakeholders to better understand the construction costs and timelines and make informed decisions. By integrating scheduling data with 3D models, project teams can simulate construction processes, identify potential issues or conflicts, and adjust as needed to optimise scheduling.

3.1.4 Environmental Information

BIM can include information on environmental factors, such as energy consumption, water usage, and carbon footprints. In addition to geometry data, such as spaces, openings, and access areas, environmental factors, such as insulation properties and glazing, can be part of BIM models. The properties of heating, ventilation, and air conditioning (HVAC) systems (Gao et al., 2019), including equipment size, efficiency ratings, airflow rates, the numbers and types of light fixtures and their wattage, and the age of plumbing fixtures, can also be added to BIM. Additionally, people-related data, such as occupancy patterns and schedules, can be included in BIM. Finally, geospatial data concerning weather conditions, such as temperature, humidity, and wind, can be integrated into BIM models.

3.1.5 Maintenance and Operations Information

In addition to data regarding the locations of systems and services within buildings and infrastructure assets, maintenance and operations information, such as condition and life cycle statuses, can be added to BIM models (Abideen et al., 2022). Data on equipment types, specifications, maintenance schedules, vendors and service providers, service level agreements, and performance metrics can also be added to BIM. Historical data on maintenance that has been performed on building systems and assets, as well as safety and compliance requirements, including fire safety, accessibility, and environmental regulations, can all be included in BIM.

3.2 Benefits of BIM

The adoption of BIM in the construction industry offers several benefits. However, these benefits go beyond those for the construction sector, which were discussed in Chapter 1 and will be discussed in the subsequent sections of this book. Some of the main benefits include improved project efficiency, reduced project costs, improved project quality, and sustainability regulatory compliance. In this section, the benefits of BIM are discussed throughout the various stages of a construction project.

3.2.1 Design and Delivery

A significant benefit of BIM in the design and delivery of buildings and infrastructure assets is its ability to provide a consolidated approach for project data, enabling project teams to collaborate and communicate more effectively and reducing errors and reworking.

BIM allows stakeholders, such as architects, engineers, contractors, and owners (Forcael et al., 2023), to share and access project data that is often kept in a centralised and cloud-based location. By providing a shared platform for project data and documentation, BIM reduces the need for face-to-face meetings and improves collaboration among stakeholders. This eliminates the need for multiple copies of the same information and ensures that all parties are working with the most up-to-date data (Roman et al., 2022). BIM can also improve coordination, reduce conflicts, and increase project efficiency by allowing stakeholders to work together digitally.

The visual representation of the construction project allows all stakeholders to understand the project better and identify potential issues, thereby reducing the likelihood of errors or conflicts (Huynh & Nguyen-Ky, 2020). The visual representation also facilitates coordination, communication, and collaboration between project stakeholders. Potential issues or conflicts can be identified early in the design process, enabling the more efficient use of resources and reducing the risk of costly mistakes.

The coordinated approach to design data, schedules (Crowther & Ajayi, 2021), cost estimates (Lu et al., 2016), and material quantities in BIM (Khosakitchalert et al., 2019) significantly facilitates informed decisions about the project scope, budget, and timeline. By simulating construction processes (Moon et al., 2014) and identifying design conflicts, BIM can help stakeholders to make necessary changes to the project and avoid costly reworking. This coordination, in turn, reduces project risk by identifying potential issues before construction begins.

3.2.2 Operation

Building management systems (BMSs) can benefit from BIM in the operation phase of building and infrastructure assets (Oti et al., 2016). BIM can be used as a digital inventory of building assets, including mechanical, electrical, and plumbing (MEP) systems, finishes, and equipment (Hu et al., 2018). This information can be used to track the condition, maintenance history, and performance of these systems over time. HVAC and lighting in BIM, for example, can be used to simulate energy performance and identify opportunities for energy savings. The time dimension in BIM can be used to schedule maintenance activities and optimise maintenance routines. By tracking the condition of systems and scheduling maintenance activities in BIM, BMSs can reduce downtime and extend the life of building assets. By feeding sensor data from BMSs into BIM, BMSs can track and visualise the occupancy and utilisation of spaces to optimise space allocation and improve utilisation, which can then be used to support emergency planning and response. By providing detailed information about building systems and layouts, BIM can help emergency responders to quickly locate critical systems and respond to emergency situations more efficiently (Tashakkori et al., 2015).

3.2.3 Beyond Buildings and Infrastructure Assets

The generalised version of data in BIM that is integrated with GIS can facilitate urban and infrastructure planning and city management. By simulating different design and infrastructure scenarios in GIS, 3D data extracted from BIM can help decision-makers to make informed decisions about urban development, optimise service delivery, and improve the quality of life for urban residents. By optimising urban design and infrastructure, BIM can help to improve urban sustainability and emergency management, as well as reducing environmental impacts (Song et al., 2017).

Urban design processes can benefit by integrating 3D models extracted from BIM with GIS. This integrated information can test the impacts of different design options on the environment, transportation, and public spaces and help to make informed decisions about urban planning and development (Xia et al., 2022).

Similar to urban design, infrastructure planning can also benefit from BIM and GIS integration. Integrated data can be used to simulate the construction and operation of urban infrastructure, such as roads, bridges, tunnels, and public transportation. By modelling different infrastructure scenarios, BIM and GIS integration can help to optimise infrastructure design, reduce construction and maintenance costs, and improve transportation efficiency and safety (Marzouk & Othman, 2020).

The integration of BIM and GIS can also be used to create digital inventories of assets, such as buildings, infrastructure, and public spaces (Garramone et al., 2020). This integration can help to track the condition, maintenance history, and performance of urban assets over time and optimise asset management strategies to reduce costs and improve service delivery.

3.3 BIM Standards

Standardisation is central in BIM as it ensures data interoperability, which is critical for effective and consistent collaboration and increased efficiency. Without a common set of standards, it becomes difficult to exchange information between stakeholders, leading to delays and misunderstandings. Standardisation also ensures consistency in the creation, management, and exchange of data. This consistency helps to ensure data accuracy, completeness, and reliability, ultimately leading to better decision-making.

From a data perspective, standardisation enables different software applications to communicate and exchange data seamlessly. This interoperability helps to avoid data loss or corruption, thereby ensuring that data are consistent and accurate throughout the project life cycle. From a process perspective, standardisation ensures that similar and consistent approaches are applied for the BIM-based design, delivery, and maintenance of buildings and infrastructure assets. Consistency also facilitates collaboration within a given project. It also ensures that methodologies can be applied in other projects, eliminating the need to develop project-specific methodologies and using lessons that have been learnt from other projects.

Many countries have regulations and codes that require certain standards for construction projects. Standardisation ensures that projects comply with these regulations, reducing the risk of costly penalties or delays. Having said that, jurisdiction-specific BIM standards are rapidly evolving, although in their early stages.

3.3.1 ISO 19650[1]

ISO 19650 is an international standard for BIM that provides guidelines for digitising information related to buildings and civil engineering works from a process perspective. The standard includes requirements for information management, the roles of stakeholders, steps and processes, and recommendations for collaboration and information exchange. It provides a framework for managing and exchanging BIM in a structured and consistent manner, ensuring that all stakeholders can access and use BIM as they need to throughout the project life cycle. The ISO 19650 standard is based on the principles of collaborative working and it covers the entire project life cycle, from the initial design phase to the construction, operation, and maintenance of the asset. The ISO 19650 standard comprises two parts:

Part 1: Concepts and Principles

This part of the standard outlines the concepts and principles of BIM and provides a framework for managing information over project life cycles. It covers topics such as collaborative working, information management processes, and the roles and responsibilities of project stakeholders.

Part 2: Delivery of the Asset

This part of the standard guides the delivery phase of projects and covers topics such as information requirements, information exchange formats, and the use of common data environments.

3.3.2 ISO 16739[2]

ISO 16739, or Industry Foundation Classes (IFC), is a file format that is used to exchange BIM between different software applications. IFC is an open standard that was developed by BuildingSMART, which is an international alliance of building industry organisations, to enable interoperability between different BIM software tools.

IFC enables software applications to share BIM with each other, regardless of the software used to create or edit the data. This improves interoperability

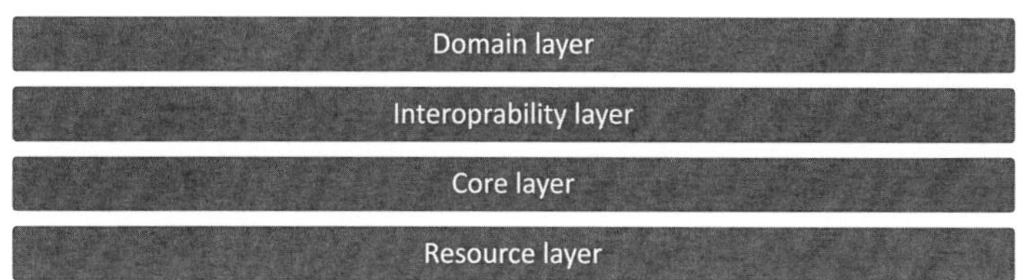

FIGURE 3.1
The four IFC layers.

between different BIM tools, enabling project teams to work more collaboratively and efficiently. It also helps to reduce errors and inconsistencies that can arise when data are transferred between different software applications using proprietary file formats. IFC provides a data model, called IFC schema, which encodes information related to building and infrastructure assets. The IFC schema is built on four layers (Figure 3.1).

The fundamental layer is called the resource layer. It is designed to include common entities. An example of information contained in the resource layer is units of measurement. The IfcMeasureResource specifies units and defined measure types that can then be assigned to quantities, such as length, area, volume, and time. The elements in this layer cannot independently exist in an IFC file. For example, unless there is a defined project, units cannot be defined in the file. Below is an example in which a project's length, area, volume, and time units are defined as SI units:

```
#1=IFCPROJECT (GlobalID, $, Name, $, $, $, $, $, #2);
#2=IFCUNITASSIGNMENT ((#3, #4, #5, #6));
#3=IFCSIUNIT (*, .LENGTHUNIT., .MILLI., .METRE.);
#4=IFCSIUNIT (*, .AREAUNIT., $, .SQUARE_METRE.);
#5=IFCSIUNIT (*, .VOLUMEUNIT., $, .CUBIC_METRE.);
#6=IFCSIUNIT (*, .TIMEUNIT., $, .SECOND.);
```

Another example is IfcShapeRepresentation, which represents particular geometric representations of building components. In the below example, a block with 1m wide, 1m deep, and 2m high is expressed using the constructive solid geometry model:

```
#1020=IFCSHAPEREPRESENTATION(#202,'Body','CSG',
  (#1021));
#1021=IFCCSGSOLID(#1022);
#1022=IFCBLOCK(#1023,1000.,1000.,2000.);
#1023=IFCAXIS2PLACEMENT3D(#1024,$,$);
#1024=IFCCARTESIANPOINT((-500.,-500.,0.));
```

The second layer of the IFC schema is called the core layer. The entities in the upper layers of the IFC schema can reference the entities in this layer. It provides the basic structure and the relationship between different entities. Using the IfcRoot of this layer, each entity outside of the resource layer gets a unique identifier, name, description, and ownership information.

This layer provides IfcObjectDefinition as a superclass to define physically tangible objects (e.g., walls), conceptual items (e.g., grids), processes (e.g., tasks), controls (e.g., cost items), resources (e.g., labour), and actors (e.g., people involved in the design process).

In the core layer, IfcPropertyDefinition is a base entity that is used to define the properties and attributes of building elements or other objects in BIM. Using IfcPropertyDefinition, we can define a set of properties that describe an object's characteristics, such as its size, shape, and material. For example, the properties of a window may be width, height, glass type, and frame material.

This layer also provides a superclass called IfcRelationship, which defines the relationship between objects. For example, a wall may be associated with a specification that defines its performance requirements. As another example, a room may be contained within a floor, which is contained within a building.

This layer also provides the means to specify objects as products, processes, or controls. Products are objects with geometries and placements within project contexts. Processes are activities or events that are ordered in time and sequenced in relation to other processes.

The next layer is called the shared element layer. This layer defines more generic entities that are commonly used in all building-related disciplines, including architecture, services, structures, and construction management. This layer defines shared buildings, services, facilities, management, and other kinds of small building parts, such as accessories and fasteners. The shared element layer is critical for interoperability between software tools, as well as collaboration and communication between different stakeholders within construction projects. Entities defined in this layer can be referenced and specialised by all of the entities above in the domain-specific IFC schema. The shared element layer provides objects and relationships that are shared by multiple domains.

The top layer in the hierarchy accommodates data elements, attributes, and relationships that are specific to particular domains or application areas, such as HVAC, electrical systems, or structural engineering. This allows for the more specialised modelling of building elements and systems and supports the exchange of more detailed and specific information between different software applications that use the IFC format. Entities defined in this layer are self-contained and cannot be referenced by any other layer. The domain-specific layer organises definitions according to industry discipline, including architecture, building automation and control, construction management, cabled systems, HVAC, plumbing and fire protection, and structural engineering.

3.3.3 Extending IFC

The IFC initiative began in 1994 and since then, it has evolved and extended. The initial version of IFC covered fewer specific schemas, while the new version provides data elements for more domains. The revisions of IFC have also improved how data are modelled. It is likely that this evolution will continue to include further improvements and extensions. There are various ways that IFC can be extended to tailor to specific applications. Some of these approaches include making changes to the core data model, while others use existing structures.

There are several extension mechanisms that can be used to extend data models in IFC without modifying the core IFC schema. These include property sets, entity attributes, and user-defined attributes. Property sets can be used to add new properties to existing IFC objects. Entity attributes can be used to define additional attributes for entities. User-defined attributes can be used to add custom attributes to any IFC entity.

The core IFC data model can also be modified and extended to accommodate domains that include other built environments, i.e., information beyond buildings. These extensions, after industry-wide consultation, can be added to the core IFC data model in the new IFC releases. Some of the non-building extensions of IFC include railways, ports, waterways, and infrastructure schemas.

Linked data is a method of publishing and connecting data on the web. By using linked data, it is possible to add information to IFC models without modifying the core schema. Linked data can also be used to connect IFC models with other sources of data, such as building product databases or environmental databases.

3.3.4 Creating, Editing, and Viewing IFC Files

There are several software tools that can be used to create and edit IFC. These tools often also provide functionalities and analytics that are required in specific domains covered in IFC.

BIM authoring tools, such as Autodesk Revit[3], Graphisoft ArchiCAD[4], and Trimble SketchUp[5], are commonly used to create and modify BIM models. These software tools provide rich functions to create BIM and generate IFC equivalents of BIM. These tools may also include features that allow users to add or modify IFC properties, create custom classes, and define new relationships.

Depending on IFC structures are understood, there are tools that allow IFC to be created and edited without directly using BIM authoring tools. The most common IFC file format is IFC-SPF, with the extension of "ifc". As explained earlier, this is a readable text format in which every object is recorded in a single line. Text editors, such as Notepad++, can create and edit IFC files.

There are also free software tools that allow users to work on IFC files directly. These include BIMvision[6], Open IFC viewer[7], and BlenderBIM[8], which provide various functions, such as visualisation, clash detection, structural analysis, and facility management.

BIM ecosystems have created open programming toolkits and libraries to build new features and functions. Some of the prominent libraries include IFC++[9] and IfcOpenShell[10]. Both of these libraries were developed based on the C++ programming language. IfcOpenShell also offers a higher-level application programming interface to deal with IFC files.

3.4 Database Management Systems for BIM

It can be argued that managing information about buildings or infrastructure assets may not require database management systems. File-based information management systems are often used when data are simple, small in size, and used by small groups who do not need to access or share it simultaneously. These file systems are not recommended when data require complex queries or include relationships that must be updated frequently or in a structured manner. These file systems are also not used when applications require high security or user access control. In most of these cases, it is justified that database approaches are required for BIM. Some software applications, such as Autodesk BIM Collaborate, enable BIM models to be managed in file-based systems while meeting the above criteria.

The use of DBMSs for BIM is an active area of research and development from two perspectives: Accommodating complex 3D geometries and relationships and developing query languages to retrieve BIM data from databases.

Existing commercial database management systems, such as Microsoft SQL Server, have been used to store IFC files. This database system can support a limited number of geometry types but often cannot accommodate the complete 3D geometries of buildings or infrastructure assets. To this end, database schemas have been developed to accommodate complex 3D geometries (Rodrigues et al., 2019).

BIM-specific database management systems have also been developed. BIMserver[11] is an open-source software solution for storing and managing IFC content in a database. The database versions, integrates, and filters data to generate IFC outputs.

QL4BIM, a query language for BIM, was developed to retrieve information about building elements, such as their geometry, attributes, relationships, and properties. It allows users to search for and filter data based on specific criteria, such as material, location, cost, or schedule.

3.5 Analysis Using BIM

BIM provides a rich source of data and information that can be analysed to extract insights and improve decision-making throughout building or infrastructure life cycles. In this section, we provide an overview of these insights.

3.5.1 Energy Analysis

BIM can be used to analyse building energy performance and identify opportunities for energy savings (Alkhatib & Mohsen Alawag, 2022). This analysis helps with better design, selecting energy-efficient equipment and systems, and identifying retrofit opportunities in existing buildings and infrastructure assets (Xu et al., 2021).

Several data elements in BIM are utilised for energy analysis. Building geometry is a critical element that provides physical characteristics, such as size, shape, and orientation. These elements help to calculate a building's surface area, volume, and thermal mass for energy analysis. Other BIM data elements, such as insulation, glazing, and construction materials used for walls, roofs, and floors, can help to analyse thermal performance and energy consumption. These elements can also help to analyse heat transfer between indoor and outdoor environments. HVAC and lighting information in BIM is also essential for energy analysis, providing information on current energy consumption. Georeferenced BIM information can also provide other essential energy analysis data, such as temperature, humidity, and solar radiation. Occupancy information, such as the number of occupants, their activities, and building use schedules, can also be included in BIM to help with modelling. There are several tools available for energy analysis using BIM, including the following:

Insight[12] and Green Building Studio[13] are energy analysis tools that use building information details to calculate energy consumption, daylighting, and thermal comfort. They can be used to evaluate different design options, simulate performance under different weather conditions, and identify opportunities for energy savings. These tools can be integrated with Revit to use BIM.

VE[14] is a building performance analysis software that can be integrated with BIM platforms, such as Revit and ArchiCAD. It offers a range of energy analysis tools, including thermal simulation, daylighting analysis, and energy code compliance.

EnergyPlus[15] is an energy simulation engine that can be used with BIM tools to simulate building energy performance and evaluate the impacts of design decisions on energy consumption. It is free, open source, and cross-platform, so it can be integrated with other software tools. For example, DesignBuilder[16] is building energy simulation software that is built on EnergyPlus but offers a more advanced user interface.

3.5.2 Structural Analysis

The data in BIM can be used to analyse buildings' structural performance, identify potential issues, and optimise structural designs. Structural analysis can help to improve building safety, reduce construction costs, and optimise material use.

Critical data for structural analysis include information regarding the load-bearing frameworks of buildings and infrastructure assets. These frameworks may include load-bearing walls, columns, beams, foundations, joints and connections, and materials, such as timber, steel, and concrete. BIM can facilitate load-bearing analysis using these structural frameworks, including dead, live, wind, and seismic loads. This framework information is not necessarily modelled in the architectural design of buildings. As such, if BIM is to be used for structural analysis, the framework components should be annotated, modelled, and integrated into architectural designs. There are tools available for structural analysis using BIM.

For example, Robot Structural Analysis[17] is a tool that can be integrated with BIM platforms, such as Revit. It can be used for the static and dynamic analysis of structural systems and supports a range of materials, including steel, concrete, and timber. Tekla Structural Designer[18] is a suite of software tools that is used for structural design, detailing, and analysis. This tool can be integrated with BIM platforms through IFC files and other proprietary formats. Similarly, SAP2000[19] is structural analysis and design software that imports exported IFC files, enabling integration with BIM ecosystems.

3.5.3 Cost Estimation and Analysis

One of the primary drivers of BIM is its ability to analyse construction costs and identify potential cost savings. Cost analysis can help to optimise building design, select the most cost-effective materials and systems, and identify areas for cost reductions.

There are several data points that help with cost analysis. These include the quantities of materials, material costs, labour costs, project schedules, and project changes. The quantities of materials required for different parts of buildings and infrastructure assets are the primary data used for cost estimation analysis. The process of calculating the quantities of materials required for construction projects is called quantity takeoff. Combined with quantity takeoff, material costs are used in BIM to calculate the required building materials. Labour costs can also be integrated into BIM as another key aspect of project costs. Construction schedules and changes can be used to manage and change orders, track costs associated with changes, and ensure that projects stay on budget.

Software tools that are used for cost estimation are often part of suites of tools for construction project management. These tools combine design and construction data for better coordination, clash resolution, and problem identification before construction starts. Navisworks and BIM 360 can be integrated with the BIM authoring tool Revit to manage projects, including cost estimation. 4D SYNCHRO Pro is project scheduling software that is built on BIM principles, which can be used for cost analysis and estimation. CostX is another BIM-based construction estimating software tool that can perform quantity takeoff and cost estimation. This tool operates based on IFC for interoperability with other BIM tools in construction software ecosystems.

3.6 Summary

This chapter introduced BIM from various perspectives. It discussed what data can be included in BIM models. The chapter also discussed the benefits of BIM in various stages of construction projects, noting that the benefits go beyond construction. It discussed BIM standards, database management systems, the types of analysis that can be done using BIM, and some of the associated software tools. The next chapter will discuss how BIM can be created for existing buildings.

Notes

1 www.iso.org/standard/68078.html
2 www.iso.org/standard/51622.html
3 www.autodesk.com.au/products/revit/overview?term=1-YEAR&tab=subscriptionIFC++
4 https://graphisoft.com/solutions/archicad
5 www.sketchup.com
6 https://bimvision.eu
7 https://openifcviewer.com
8 https://blenderbim.org
9 https://ifcquery.com
10 https://ifcopenshell.org
11 https://bimserver.org
12 www.autodesk.com/products/insight/overview
13 https://gbs.autodesk.com/GBS/
14 www.iesve.com/software/virtual-environment
15 https://energyplus.net
16 https://designbuilder.com.au

17 www.autodesk.com.au/products/robot-structural-analysis/overview
18 www.tekla.com/products/tekla-structural-designer#SA
19 www.csiamerica.com/products/sap2000

Bibliography

Abideen, D. K., Yunusa-Kaltungo, A., Manu, P., & Cheung, C. (2022). A systematic review of the extent to which BIM is integrated into operation and maintenance. *Sustainability (Switzerland)*, *14*(14). https://doi.org/10.3390/su14148692

Alkhatib, F., & Mohsen Alawag, A. (2022). Building Information Modelling (BIM) and energy performance of building – A review. *Journal of Applied Artificial Intelligence*, *2*(1). https://doi.org/10.48185/jaai.v2i1.581

Azhar, S., Khalfan, M., & Maqsood, T. (2012). Building information modeling (BIM): Now and beyond. *Australasian Journal of Construction Economics and Building*, *12*(4). https://doi.org/10.5130/ajceb.v12i4.3032

Boton, C., Kubicki, S., & Halin, G. (2015). The challenge of level of development in 4D/BIM simulation across AEC project lifecyle. A case study. *Procedia Engineering*, *123*. https://doi.org/10.1016/j.proeng.2015.10.058

Crowther, J., & Ajayi, S. O. (2021). Impacts of 4D BIM on construction project performance. *International Journal of Construction Management*, *21*(7). https://doi.org/10.1080/15623599.2019.1580832

Eadie, R., Browne, M., Odeyinka, H., McKeown, C., & McNiff, S. (2013). BIM implementation throughout the UK construction project lifecycle: An analysis. *Automation in Construction*, *36*. https://doi.org/10.1016/j.autcon.2013.09.001

Forcael, E., Puentes, C., García-Alvarado, R., Opazo-Vega, A., Soto-Muñoz, J., & Moroni, G. (2023). Profile characterization of building information modeling users. *Buildings*, *13*(1). https://doi.org/10.3390/buildings13010060

Gao, H., Koch, C., & Wu, Y. (2019). Building information modelling based building energy modelling: A review. *Applied Energy*, *238*. https://doi.org/10.1016/j.apenergy.2019.01.032

Garramone, M., Moretti, N., Scaioni, M., Ellul, C., Re Cecconi, F., & Dejaco, M. C. (2020). BIM and GIS integration for infrastructure asset management : A bibliometric analysis. *ISPRS Annals of the Photogrammetry, Remote Sensing and Spatial Information Sciences*, *6*(4/W1). https://doi.org/10.5194/isprs-annals-VI-4-W1-2020-77-2020

Hu, Z. Z., Tian, P. L., Li, S. W., & Zhang, J. P. (2018). BIM-based integrated delivery technologies for intelligent MEP management in the operation and maintenance phase. *Advances in Engineering Software*, *115*. https://doi.org/10.1016/j.advengsoft.2017.08.007

Huynh, D., & Nguyen-Ky, S. (2020). Engaging building automation data visualisation using building information modelling and progressive web application. *Open Engineering*, *10*(1). https://doi.org/10.1515/eng-2020-0054

Khosakitchalert, C., Yabuki, N., & Fukuda, T. (2019). Improving the accuracy of BIM-based quantity takeoff for compound elements. *Automation in Construction*, *106*. https://doi.org/10.1016/j.autcon.2019.102891

Latiffi, A. A., Brahim, J., Mohd, S., & Fathi, M. S. (2015). Building Information Modeling (BIM): Exploring Level of Development (LOD) in construction projects. *Applied Mechanics and Materials*, *773–774*. https://doi.org/10.4028/www.scientific.net/amm.773-774.933

Lu, Q., Won, J., & Cheng, J. C. P. (2016). A financial decision making framework for construction projects based on 5D Building Information Modeling (BIM). *International Journal of Project Management*, *34*(1). https://doi.org/10.1016/j.ijproman.2015.09.004

Marzouk, M., & Othman, A. (2020). Planning utility infrastructure requirements for smart cities using the integration between BIM and GIS. *Sustainable Cities and Society*, *57*. https://doi.org/10.1016/j.scs.2020.102120

Moon, H., Kim, H., Kim, C., & Kang, L. (2014). Development of a schedule-workspace interference management system simultaneously considering the overlap level of parallel schedules and workspaces. *Automation in Construction*, *39*. https://doi.org/10.1016/j.autcon.2013.06.001

Oti, A. H., Kurul, E., Cheung, F., & Tah, J. H. M. (2016). A framework for the utilization of building management system data in building information models for building design and operation. *Automation in Construction*, *72*. https://doi.org/10.1016/j.autcon.2016.08.043

Rodrigues, F., Teixeira, J., Matos, R., & Rodrigues, H. (2019). Development of a web application for historical building management through BIM technology. *Advances in Civil Engineering*, *2019*. https://doi.org/10.1155/2019/9872736

Roman, A., Andrii, S., Galyna, R., Honcharenko, T., Iurii, C., & Hanna, S. (2022). Integration of data flows of the construction project life cycle to create a digital enterprise based on building information modeling. *International Journal of Emerging Technology and Advanced Engineering*, *12*(1). https://doi.org/10.46338/IJETAE0122_05

Song, Y., Wang, X., Tan, Y., Wu, P., Sutrisna, M., Cheng, J. C. P., & Hampson, K. (2017). Trends and opportunities of BIM-GIS integration in the architecture, engineering and construction industry: A review from a spatio-temporal statistical perspective. *ISPRS International Journal of Geo-Information*, *6*(12). https://doi.org/10.3390/ijgi6120397

Tashakkori, H., Rajabifard, A., & Kalantari, M. (2015). A new 3D indoor/outdoor spatial model for indoor emergency response facilitation. *Building and Environment*, *89*. https://doi.org/10.1016/j.buildenv.2015.02.036

Xia, H., Liu, Z., Efremochkina, M., Liu, X., & Lin, C. (2022). Study on city digital twin technologies for sustainable smart city design: A review and bibliometric analysis of geographic information system and building information modeling integration. *Sustainable Cities and Society*, *84*. https://doi.org/10.1016/j.scs.2022.104009

Xu, X., Mumford, T., & Zou, P. X. W. (2021). Life-cycle building information modelling (BIM) engaged framework for improving building energy performance. *Energy and Buildings*, *231*. https://doi.org/10.1016/j.enbuild.2020.110496

4

Creating BIM Using 3D Laser Scanning

4.1 Introduction

In BIM, the integration of 3D laser scanning technology has revolutionised how buildings and infrastructure are surveyed, modelled, and managed. This chapter explores the methodologies behind using 3D laser scanning to create georeferenced BIM, encompassing various survey processes and best practices for seamless integration.

The evolution of surveying technology has seen a paradigm shift since the advent of 3D laser scanning. Traditional surveying methods, while effective, often entail time-consuming processes and limitations in terms of capturing detailed spatial information. In contrast, 3D laser scanning offers a rapid and highly accurate means of capturing complex geometries and spatial data, making it indispensable in the realm of BIM.

Additionally, 3D laser scanning enables a myriad of survey processes that contribute to the creation of BIM. From capturing detailed point-cloud data for both internal and external building structures to facilitating accurate measurements and as-built documentation, the versatility of 3D laser scanning streamlines surveying workflows and enhances the quality and precision of BIM models.

A holistic approach is essential to ensure the accuracy of 3D laser scanning for BIM creation. This encompasses systematic methodologies comprising several stages:

- Establishing robust survey control networks to facilitate the seamless scanning of building interiors and exteriors, while ensuring georeferencing;
- Implementing calibration methodologies for laser scanning equipment to optimise data acquisition and accuracy;
- Conducting the comprehensive scanning of sites and buildings by employing suitable scanning techniques and parameters to capture detailed spatial information;
- Processing scanning outputs using advanced software tools to generate precise point-cloud data;

DOI: 10.1201/9781351200950-4

- Assessing the quality of scanning outputs through rigorous validation and verification processes to ensure data integrity and accuracy;
- Utilising the processed point-cloud data to create detailed and accurate BIM models, incorporating geometric, spatial, and attribute information.

This chapter presents comprehensive Scan-to-BIM guidelines. These guidelines serve as a framework for practitioners and researchers, offering a standardised approach to leveraging 3D laser scanning technology for seamless integration into BIM workflows. By following these guidelines, the efficiency, accuracy, and utility of 3D laser scanning in BIM creation can be optimised, thereby advancing the fields of digital construction and infrastructure management.

4.2 Establishing Seamless 3D Survey Control Networks

Seamless indoor and outdoor 3D survey networks can facilitate the creation of georeferenced BIM from lidar data. To this end, it is recommended that conventional land surveying approaches are combined with global navigation satellite system approaches or levelling methods for measurements to set up 3D networks of the exteriors of buildings (Figure 4.1).

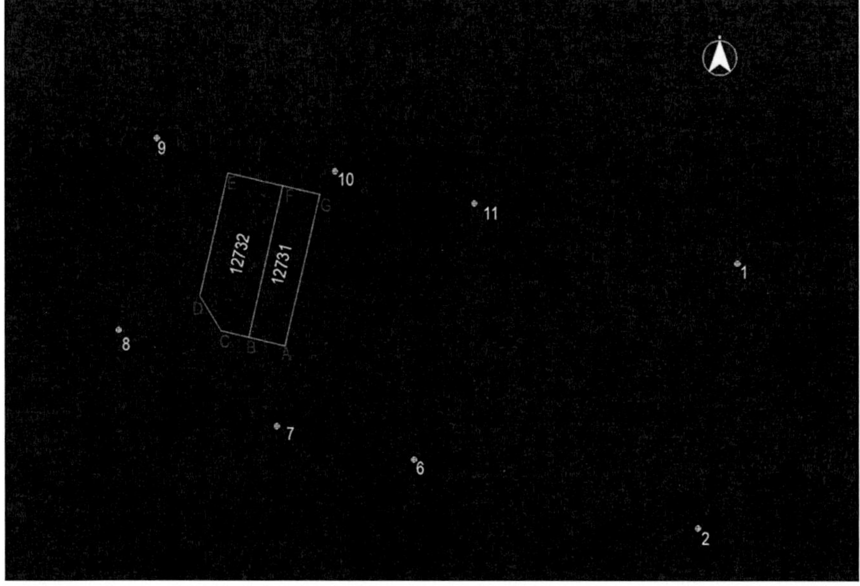

FIGURE 4.1
A network of control points (CPs) set up for laser scanning.

FIGURE 4.2
Building footprint and roof edge survey.

Using control points (CPs) within these networks, the coordinates for the boundary points of the land that contains the buildings, the building footprints, and the edges of rooftops can be calculated (Figure 4.2). This information is critical for the accurate georeferencing of BIM. Trigonometric surveys can also be used to determine and transfer horizontal (E, N) and vertical (height) data from exterior to interior CPs.

Establishing survey control networks for the interiors of buildings is also helpful. The 3D trigonometric surveying method can be used to transfer coordinates from exterior networks of CPs to the interiors of buildings.

Interior CPs must be selected based on two principles (see the black circles in Figure 4.3). First, every CP should have a line of sight to three other CPs. The first principle is to meet the redundancy required for survey networks. Second, the CPs in each space should have a line of sight to the space's architectural components (i.e., walls, doors, and windows). The second principle is to minimise the impact of occlusions. However, for well-furnished buildings, spaces to place 3D scanners can be limited due to the obstruction of furniture.

Using networks of targets in the interiors (see the red circles in Figure 4.3) and exteriors of buildings is also recommended for 3D laser scanning. These targets can be used for two purposes. First, they can be used to register scans in case the processing software's automatic registration is not successful. Second, they can be used as 3D control points for measuring uncertainty in laser scanning outputs.

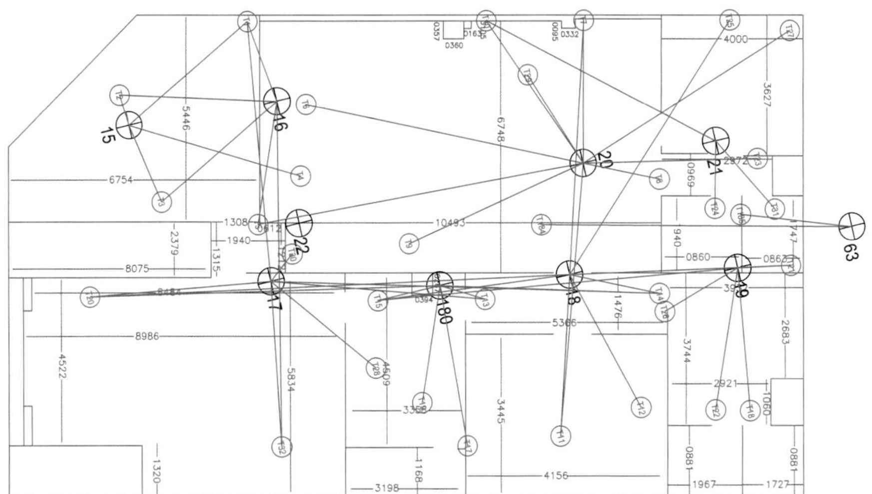

FIGURE 4.3
Distribution of control points and targets inside a building.

4.3 Scanning Buildings

Several types of 3D laser scanning technologies are commonly used for surveying and mapping. These technologies vary in their scanning principles, ranges, accuracy, and applications.

Airborne laser scanning uses laser scanners mounted on aircraft or drones to capture high-density 3D point-cloud data of large areas from above. It is widely used for topographic mapping and vegetation management. Mobile laser scanning utilises laser scanners mounted on vehicles or drones to capture 3D point-cloud data while moving through built environments. It offers rapid data acquisition over large areas and is well-suited for urban mapping, infrastructure management, and transportation surveys.

Terrestrial laser scanning involves using stationary laser scanners positioned at various locations around buildings to capture detailed 3D point-cloud data. It provides high-resolution scans of building exteriors and interiors, making it suitable for architectural documentation and structural analysis. Handheld laser scanning involves the use of portable laser scanners held by operators to capture 3D point-cloud data in confined or complex indoor spaces. It offers flexibility and manoeuvrability for the detailed scanning of building interiors, making it ideal for architectural preservation, renovation, and facility management. In this section, we expand on the use of terrestrial and handheld devices as suitable methods for creating BIM.

4.3.1 Handheld Devices

Handheld devices are lightweight and user-friendly. They allow users to scan environments while walking. They are built based on simultaneous localisation and mapping method (SLAM) technology. The SLAM method processes raw scan data into point clouds using a method that is analogous to the traverse technique used in land surveying in that previously known positions are used to determine the current position.

SLAM refers to the process through which a device that is placed in an unknown environment can incrementally construct a map of this environment whilst simultaneously using this map to deduce its trajectory and position (Bailey & Durrant-Whyte, 2006; Durrant-Whyte & Bailey, 2006).

SLAM is commonly utilised in the field of autonomous robotics, aiming to eliminate the human-guided navigation of robots, but SLAM processes have also been utilised in handheld laser scanners controlled by human operators, which can map and generate detailed 3D point clouds of unknown environments whilst keeping track of their positions.

SLAM relies on estimating the positions of distinct features within environments for successful device localisation and mapping. However, unrecognised associations between observations and features lead to uncertainty in the devices' positioning, wherein the device can pick wrong data associations, resulting in divergence in the mapping (Li et al., 2020). In this regard, the lack of distinctive features in an environment can lead to poorer mapping performance from SLAM-based mobile laser scanners.

As such, SLAM-based methods can compound introduced errors, causing measured positions to "drift". When using handheld devices for surveys, it is a good practice to "close the loop" by re-surveying known positions to adjust any compounded errors around the loop. When using any SLAM method, as a minimum, the operator is required to start and end the survey in the same position to ensure at least one loop closure. Feature-rich environments help to obtain more accurate outputs when using SLAM-based method. As such, when scanning environments do not contain many objects, this may result in less accurate mapping.

When transitioning from enclosed, feature-rich environments to open, feature-poor environments (for example, when exiting a building), errors may be introduced. If no other features are within range, it may be necessary to turn and face the exit and the exterior of the building.

When using handheld devices, it is recommended to start scanning from the exteriors of buildings if there are no networks of CPs.

When using handheld devices, data are better captured at a slow pace to ensure proper coverage and high-resolution data. When transitioning to the interior of a building using a doorway, it is recommended to slow down to ensure there is a period when the scanner can view features on both sides of the doorway. The same principle needs to be practised when transitioning through staircases whilst scanning multistorey buildings. After the scanning is finished, the project closes the scanning loop by coming back to the start point.

SLAM technology does not rely on targets or control points. However, some handheld devices contain technologies for georeferencing. By using time in the scanning trajectory, these scanners can recognise when they have stopped motion. Based on this feature, with the help of reference plates, scanners can be set up on control points to increase the accuracy of data collection. During scanning, control points can be located precisely using reference plates. These plates are used to simplify the georeferencing process. During scanning, the scanners need to be set up on control points, using reference plates, for a 5-second time period.

Scanning using handheld devices should be broken down into multiple scanning missions for extensive surveys, such as multistorey buildings. This split is to avoid large file sizes and reduce any drifts that may be created in the scanned data. It is recommended that each survey is limited to 30 minutes.

When using handheld devices, the data quality can be impacted by fast 180° turns and extreme motion in the environment. An essential prerequisite for using handheld devices is route planning, e.g., propping open doors along the route and making sure that people are stationary for the duration of the scan. It is better to start scanning with large rooms that are connected to many hallways. When reaching turning points, the operator must move the scanner carefully to a vertical position and maintain that position until the turns are complete.

It is difficult to obtain sound outputs for spaces that have insufficient light for handheld devices equipped with cameras, such as staircases. Scanning spaces that have significant height changes in a given distance, such as stairs, can also be problematic for handheld devices. It is recommended that these spaces are scanned separately from corresponding flat areas. It is also recommended that overlaps are obtained between the stairs on each floor and then the scans can be registered afterwards to prevent losing track. Walking down stairs to scan them is recommended because the angles are better for simultaneous localisation.

4.3.2 Terrestrial Laser Scanners

Terrestrial laser scanners are scanners that are mounted on tripods and have fixed positions while collecting data. Terrestrial laser scanners are often equipped with imaging systems. They can collect data in the form of full-colour images overlaid on point clouds. Two classes of scanners can be used to scan buildings: Short-range and medium-range scanners.

The selection of scanning positions and overlapping areas is critical for terrestrial scanners. Also, it is essential to understand the amount of coverage that is required to create BIM. Restricted or no access areas impact what can be modelled. In the scanning process, it is crucial to reduce the distance between two adjacent scanning positions and avoid disturbance from sunlight when scanning.

Short-range devices are small and lightweight. They also have a lower density in terms of the number of points that they collect, as well as lower-quality imaging systems. The field methodology for these devices often does not use control points as the setup stations. The reason for this is that the standard tripods for these devices are not equipped with optical plump bobs (Figure 4.4). In these cases, the scanners need to be set up to have a clear line of sight to the CPs so that the CPs can be used for georeferencing in the registration process.

In addition to their higher-density point-cloud collection, medium-range terrestrial laser scanners are equipped with higher-resolution cameras that can obtain images at high speeds. The scanning time per station using these devices can be as short as 3 minutes. Scanning approaches using medium-range scanners can use CPs.

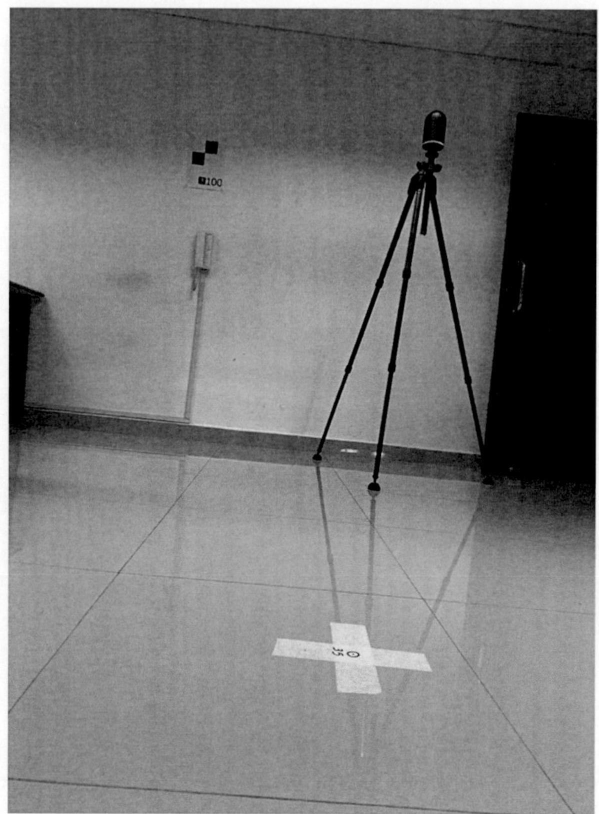

FIGURE 4.4
A tripod that is not equipped with an optical plump bob.

4.3.3 Calibration Methodologies

The calibration of laser scanners can entail two components: Calibration by the manufacturers and a calibration field established by an authority.

It is recommended that laser scanners used for BIM are sent to their manufacturers for periodic calibration and certification to enhance their performance and accuracy. Most manufacturers provide annual certification as part of their warranty plans. The calibration should include the adjustment of internal sensors (such as distance, intensity, and temperature sensors), altimeter tests, GNSS tests (when applicable), inclinometer tests, and colour tests.

It is recommended that calibration fields be established for BIM. While most calibration methodologies use point-based approaches, plane-based approaches are suggested for BIM. The reason for using plane-based approaches is that the significant features of BIM are planar features, such as walls, ceilings, and floors. Therefore, it is critical for the parameters of scanners to be optimised based on planar references.

To select a calibration field, using a 60-sqm room with the typical height of an apartment, e.g., 3–3.5 metres, is recommended. Several calibration panels (1.0m x 1.5m) should be distributed in the test room to cover the space as completely as possible.

Using laser scanning, a large number of observations (in the x, y, and z planes) can be collected and the parameters for the planes, the scanner positions, and the scanner calibration can be calculated. For terrestrial laser scanners, it is recommended that four separate, evenly distributed instrumental positions with varying heights are used.

4.4 Processing Point Clouds

Original data collected from field measurements should be processed before modelling. Scans that were taken at different positions need to be merged, which is called registration. The processing phase may also include simplifying and downsizing, removing noise, and clearing the data of unnecessary features.

There are various methods for simplifying point clouds, with most falling into two main categories: Mesh-based simplification and direct simplification. Mesh-based simplification works by building irregular meshes based on point clouds and then removing redundant meshes via a given rule to simplify the point clouds, whereas direct simplification works to simplify point clouds by analysing their characteristics (Ji et al., 2019).

Some existing direct simplification methods include Octree (Song et al., 2017), spatial indexing (Shi et al., 2022), and space bounding boxes (Fuqun

& Hui, 2022), although most direct simplification methods struggle with retaining important features in point clouds (Ji et al., 2019).

Ji et al. (2019) proposed a simplification method, called the detail feature points simplified algorithm, which is based on the importance of points. This method calculates and uses four characteristic operators to determine the importance of points: The normal vector difference, the projection distance, the spatial distance, and the curvature difference. Points that are found to be over a certain threshold for importance are retained entirely, while remaining points are simplified using an Octree method.

Most laser scanner manufacturers provide point-cloud processing and registration tools. The processing step is typically as follows: Multiple scans are uploaded and then the operator specifies parameters to align the scans and start processing. The parameters facilitating registration include control points, targets, and cloud-to-cloud registration, considering horizontal and vertical overlaps. In terms of registration, adequate overlapping areas are the most significant determinant. The larger the overlapping area, the more effortless the data merging. Also, the selection of scanning positions significantly influences the quality of overlapping areas.

There are often a few options for georeferencing. It can be undertaken scan by scan: When each scan is registered, control points are identified and their corresponding geographic coordinates are added to them for georeferencing. Another option is for control points to be added after all of the scans are registered into a single model and that single model then is georeferenced. It is recommended to have at least four georeferenced target points and one control point. This provides enough redundancy for the dismissal of control or target points if they happen to introduce errors.

Handheld devices with inbuilt technology that facilitates georeferencing require a longer processing time. In the processing stage, the inbuilt software uses the time period as an indication of the existence of control points. After the data are registered, the identified control points in the scans can be georeferenced using the coordinates derived for 3D survey networks.

4.5 Assessing the Accuracy of Scanning Outputs

The quality of BIM depends on the laser scanning survey outputs, as well as the process of converting surveys into BIM. Concerning laser scanning surveys for BIM purposes, the accuracy of the laser scanning surveys can be influenced by several underlying factors, such as the laser scanning technology, the accuracy of the survey control network, the accuracy of the individual instrumentation being used, and the accuracy when registering the individual laser scans onto the control framework.

There are evaluation frameworks for benchmarking indoor modelling methods (Khoshelham et al., 2018), which include three criteria that provide a quantitative measure of the geometric quality of indoor models: Completeness, correctness, and accuracy. These criteria are compared relative to reference models. This requires having ground truth measurements to ensure the quality of BIM.

Density and accuracy have tended to be the main parameters used to evaluate the quality of point clouds (Rebolj et al., 2017), although the direct relation between these parameters and the success of Scan-to-BIM is inconclusive. Rebolj et al. (2017) suggested a method that provides more quantitative measures of quality, namely surface coverage and depth accuracy.

Regardless of the evaluation method, ground truth data are required to assess the quality of scanning outputs concerning BIM dimensions. Often, buildings have floor plans that can be used as ground truth data for the evaluation of point-cloud accuracy. Alternatively, distometers can be used to measure the dimensions of building interiors if building plans do not exist. Several dimensions must be measured to assess the accuracy of scanning outputs.

These dimensions are compared against the corresponding distances in the reference data. For each scanned space, the absolute (A_e) and relative (R_e) errors of the measurements should be calculated to evaluate the quality of the scanning process against conventional methods.

$$A_e = true_d - model_d \tag{1}$$

$$R_e = \frac{A_e}{true_d} \tag{2}$$

$$MRE = \frac{\sum_{i=1}^{n}(R_e i)}{n} \tag{3}$$

$$RMSE = \sqrt{\frac{\sum_{i=1}^{n}(A_e i)^2}{n}} \tag{4}$$

In recent years, there have been extensive case studies and analysis papers on topics such as utilising multisource and multitemporal data (Ghamisi et al., 2018) and fusing stereo-image point clouds and lidar point clouds (Yang et al., 2017). The concept of integration in these works covers a wide range of topics, from pan sharpening and spatiospectral data fusion to more complex workflows for point-cloud classification and interpolating RGB colour algorithms.

There are techniques for integrating different datasets (Chhatkuli et al., 2015), such using 3D models generated from aerial images and mobile laser scanning. These techniques suggest that the integration of data from multiple sensors can add more information to and reduce uncertainty in data processing. The integration of multisensory data compensates for the uncertainty in each type of data and helps to create more detailed and more accurate 3D models.

These works have laid solid foundations and developed workflows for how to make use of multiple data sources to improve scanning results. To this end, it is possible to increase BIM accuracy and completeness by integrating scans from handheld and terrestrial devices. Different scanners offer different levels of accuracy and completeness in captured data. Hence, data integration presents the opportunity to cover for the shortcomings of each type of scanner (i.e., occlusion in terrestrial laser scanners and noise in handheld scanners), potentially improving BIM outputs.

Noise in data can be removed by referencing data that are of higher quality instead of simply applying noise removal methods, such as the mean distance outlier. In other words, as an alternative to using common statistical outlier removal methods, which compute mean distance estimation to identify outliers of standalone clouds, separate and cleaner datasets can be used as a benchmark to filter out noise from lower-quality data via cloud-to-cloud algorithms. Having said that, cleaning point clouds using noise removal methods can significantly hinder the completeness of BIM. In other words, BIM may end up being incomplete for a small gain in RMSE (Figure 4.5).

4.6 Creating BIM from Point Clouds

Currently, 3D scans from laser scanners that output point-cloud data have to undergo long and tedious processes to be usable in various industries, including land surveying. For point-cloud data to be usable, objects of interest must be identified, extracted, and digitally drawn in computer-aided design (CAD) or BIM environments.

BIM authoring tools, such as Revit, are used to create BIM. There are also state-of-the-art automatic Scan-to-BIM software tools[1] that can facilitate the creation of BIM. These tools apply automatic and semi-automatic approaches to converting point clouds into BIM. These tools input 3D scan data and output 3D models.

It is important to note that the outputs of these tools require quality checks to remove potential mismatches between input 3D scan data and output data. When using these tools, there may be issues in creating BIM

FIGURE 4.5
Incorrect orientation of walls in BIM, generated from simplified point-cloud data (right).

if the software that is processing the point-cloud data for registration does not reduce the data to approximate the planar surfaces of architectural components (Figure 4.6).

While there are data that are representative of features in collected data, the density of point clouds may not be enough for the automatic extraction of these features. Reflective surfaces, such as large windows, adversely impact data collection. Automatic solutions can also model elements that are not logically associated with buildings. These elements can be introduced as false positives in automatic modelling.

It is essential to note that the completeness of BIM models generated from cleaned point-cloud inputs may be reduced. Since not all noise removal processes can distinguish between or classify significant elements in BIM, such as walls and furniture, key elements may be incorrectly removed from raw point clouds during the cleaning process. This leads to fewer features being confidently identified and classified in the modelling process, resulting in BIM models with reduced completeness. Whilst manual noise removal from point clouds can produce more accurate point clouds, it imposes an extra manual operation.

a

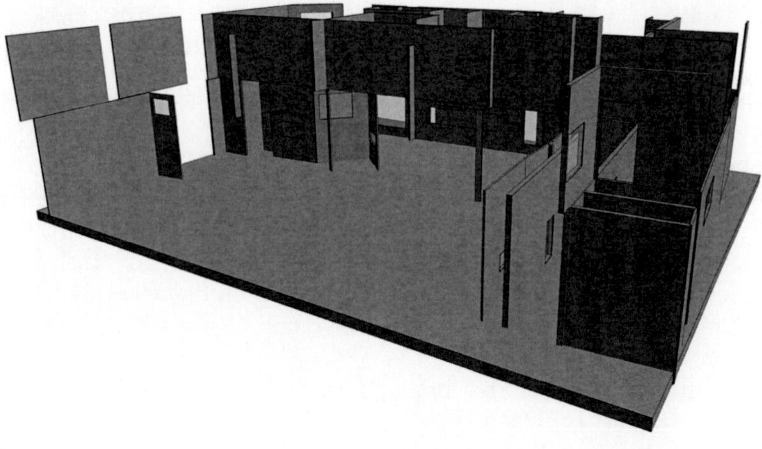

b

FIGURE 4.6
A comparison of BIM measurements generated (a) point-cloud data, (b) an automatic solution, and (c) manually modelled BIM.

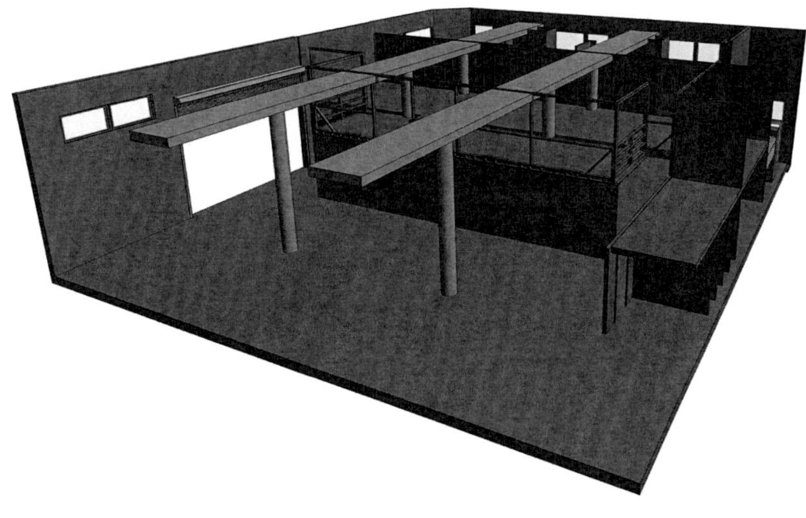

c

FIGURE 4.6 (Continued)

4.7 Commercial and Technical Considerations in Scan-to-BIM

Four critical criteria are suggested for selecting appropriate methodologies for Scan-to-BIM, which cover commercial and technical considerations. The commercial factors include the costs of purchasing laser scanning devices, the costs of purchasing the associated software tools, the costs of fieldwork (including labour, setup, and data collection), and the costs of office work (including labour, data processing, and planning). The technical factors include the accuracy of the devices' outputs and the quality of the data processing for building modelling.

4.7.1 Costs of Purchasing Devices and Associated Software Tools

The cost of an instrument is a defining business factor. Handheld devices are generally more affordable than terrestrial devices. This difference is attributed to the wider utility of terrestrial scanners in more application domains, considering different ranges, accuracy, and data demands. From an investment perspective, terrestrial scanners are recommended for engineering surveying and similar areas. However, handheld devices are more suitable for applications like indoor modelling, which require flexibility of movement in confined spaces, such as spaces containing building services or underground applications. Terrestrial devices can also be used by surveying firms in more applications than handheld devices.

4.7.2 Fieldwork

Fieldwork, including preparation, setup, and data collection, is another critical business factor in surveying. For georeferenced BIM, this includes first re-establishing and confirming existing surveys/networks in relation to buildings. This work includes measurements like sets of control points used in previous surveys to and boundary corners of the land. Georeferenced BIM then involves measuring land boundaries in relation to building structures, most commonly walls.

Regardless of the laser scanning method, the first part of fieldwork needs to be undertaken per the conventional approach for a geo-referenced BIM. A 3D survey network is required to be established to geo-reference the point cloud data collected using laser scanning. The 3D survey network takes a significant amount of time.

The point of differentiation between scanning devices is the data collection stage. In this stage, handheld devices are operator-friendly. Using terrestrial laser scanners, meanwhile, is an elaborate approach for indoor scanning. For BIM, scanning for about 3-5 minutes per station is required, depending on the device.

4.7.3 Point-Cloud Data Processing

Data processing includes preparing databases to contain point-cloud data, importing data, and registering point clouds. Data processing is, in general, a semi-automated process that requires the supervision of an operator. The duration of data processing is closely correlated with the duration of data collection.

Processing data from handled devices is much faster than processing data from terrestrial laser scanners. While there are software tools that can, to a large extent, register laser scanning data automatically, there is a need for an operator to supervise this registration to identify and align scans that the software cannot process.

4.7.4 Point-Cloud Data Quality

Data quality, regarding dimensional errors, in terrestrial laser scanning is better than that in handheld devices. This is expected and aligns with the declared accuracy of the devices by the manufacturers. The integrity of the data is defined in terms of being able to extract architectural features that are important for BIM. While point clouds representing architectural features can be captured and seen in point clouds, the extracted features from handheld devices may not be as accurate as those from terrestrial devices due to the density of the data and noise in the data. This is attributed to the processing ability of the software tools that accompany terrestrial devices.

4.8 Best Practice for Scan-to-BIM

Comprehensive laser scanning approaches are broken into five distinct stages: Re-establishing land boundaries; establishing 3D survey networks, including control points and scanning targets; scanning building interiors and exteriors; data processing, including georeferencing point clouds; and creating BIM using the processed point clouds.

Re-establishing the land boundaries of buildings involves resurveying the boundary points by connecting to a set of existing control points and using previous surveys. Establishing 3D survey networks, including building interiors and exteriors, is the most elaborate part of these methodologies.

The time spent scanning building interiors and exteriors varies based on the choice of devices. Scanning using handheld devices is often much faster than using terrestrial methods. The time spent processing, including georeferencing, is closely associated with the time taken for scanning. The processing stage includes setting up databases and importing data in preparation for the processing work.

The final stage of these approaches includes creating BIM by extracting the required data. For the creation of detailed BIM, handheld device outputs may not offer the required quality. For example, some features, such as windows, may not be acutely identifiable. On the other hand, the outputs of terrestrial devices are higher quality, enabling the extraction of most features.

Best practice is to utilise the stages that potentially create productivity and remove or modify the stages that introduce burdens compared to conventional approaches.

The land boundary re-establishment stage is essential for georeferencing and, regardless of the scanning device, it needs to be done similarly as it is a requirement of cadastral surveying.

It has been noted that establishing 3D survey networks of CPs for building interiors and setting up terrestrial devices on those CPs is significantly burdensome. This implies that introducing laser scanning potentially introduces more burdens than conventional approaches.

To optimise the measurement stage, it is suggested that established 3D networks be restricted to building exteriors. Exterior 3D survey networks facilitate the georeferencing of buildings in relation to 3D data. For this, 3D scans of building exteriors are taken and then georeferenced in the processing stage.

It is recommended that the interiors of buildings are scanned without any internal control points. These scans can be registered to exterior scans using cloud-to-cloud registration. This approach results in georeferenced point clouds of buildings. This approach saves significant time and effort by removing the 3D network establishment stage.

Another significant burden can be observed in the use of terrestrial devices. Whether using established 3D networks to guide the scanning or adopting control network-free methods, scanning using terrestrial devices requires significantly longer periods of time than scanning using handheld devices. On the other hand, handheld laser scanners offer efficiency by reducing the scanning time.

Having said that, the data outputs of handheld laser scanning devices can present issues in representing and extracting interior environments. The processing software tools that accompany handheld devices sometimes output ill-structured data and noise, requiring more processing.

Finally, BIM creation can be facilitated using automated Scan-to-BIM software solutions. The outputs of these automatic approaches require quality assurance to ensure that the generated models address false positives and true negatives.

Key points to consider in Scan-to-BIM methodologies include the following:

1. Whether handheld or terrestrial devices output point clouds that meet the requirements of BIM;
2. While terrestrial devices' outputs are more accurate than those of handheld devices, using them adds a significant extra burden to fieldwork;
3. Setting up 3D control networks in building interiors imposes a significant extra burden;
4. The quality of point clouds from terrestrial devices, in terms of geometry and integrity, is more suitable for the creation of BIM; however, the time required to process terrestrial laser scanner data is four times that of handheld scanners;
5. The outputs of handheld devices are suitable for BIM features, such as walls and ceilings;
6. The automatic conversation of point clouds into BIM yields significant efficiency in data processing.

4.9 Summary

This chapter presented comprehensive Scan-to-BIM guidelines. It offered an overview of methodologies, including creating survey control networks, calibration, the scanning of sites and buildings, processing scans, assessing scanning quality, and utilising processed point clouds to create BIM. By following these guidelines, the efficiency, accuracy, and utility of 3D laser scanning in BIM creation can be optimised, thereby advancing the fields of digital construction and infrastructure management. In the next chapter, we discuss georeferencing considerations for 3D models that are not positioned in geographical contexts.

Note

1 www.faramoon.io, https://pointfuse.com, and www.faro.com/en/Products/Software/As-BuiltTM-Software

Bibliography

Bailey, T., & Durrant-Whyte, H. (2006). Simultaneous localization and mapping (SLAM): Part II. *IEEE Robotics and Automation Magazine, 13*(3). https://doi.org/10.1109/MRA.2006.1678144

Chhatkuli, S., Satoh, T., & Tachibana, K. (2015). Multi sensor data integration for an accurate 3D model generation. *International Archives of the Photogrammetry, Remote Sensing and Spatial Information Sciences – ISPRS Archives, 40*(4W5). https://doi.org/10.5194/isprsarchives-XL-4-W5-103-2015

Durrant-Whyte, H., & Bailey, T. (2006). Simultaneous localization and mapping: Part I. *IEEE Robotics and Automation Magazine, 13*(2). https://doi.org/10.1109/MRA.2006.1638022

Fuqun, Z., & Hui, T. (2022). Hierarchical simplification algorithm for scattered point clouds. *Laser and Optoelectronics Progress, 59*(18). https://doi.org/10.3788/LOP202259.1811006

Ghamisi, P., Behnood R., Naoto Y., Qunming W. Bernhard H., Lorenzo B., Francesca B., et al. (2018). Multisource and multitemporal data fusion in remote sensing. *arXiv preprint arXiv:1812.08287*.

Ji, C., Li, Y., Fan, J., & Lan, S. (2019). A novel simplification method for 3D geometric point cloud based on the importance of point. *IEEE Access, 7*. https://doi.org/10.1109/ACCESS.2019.2939684

Khoshelham, K., Tran, H., Díaz-Vilariño, L., Peter, M., Kang, Z., & Acharya, D. (2018). An evaluation framework for benchmarking indoor modelling methods. *International Archives of the Photogrammetry, Remote Sensing and Spatial Information Sciences – ISPRS Archives, 42*(4). https://doi.org/10.5194/isprs-archives-XLII-4-297-2018

Li, Y., Brasch, N., Wang, Y., Navab, N., & Tombari, F. (2020). Structure-SLAM: Low-drift monocular SLAM in indoor environments. *IEEE Robotics and Automation Letters, 5*(4). https://doi.org/10.1109/LRA.2020.3015456

Rebolj, D., Pučko, Z., Babič, N. Č., Bizjak, M., & Mongus, D. (2017). Point cloud quality requirements for Scan-vs-BIM based automated construction progress monitoring. *Automation in Construction, 84*. https://doi.org/10.1016/j.autcon.2017.09.021

Shi, Z., Xu, W., & Meng, H. (2022). A point cloud simplification algorithm based on weighted feature indexes for 3D scanning sensors. *Sensors, 22*(19). https://doi.org/10.3390/s22197491

Song, S., Liu, J., & Yin, C. (2017). Data reduction for point cloud using octree coding. *Lecture Notes in Computer Science (Including Subseries Lecture Notes in Artificial*

Intelligence and Lecture Notes in Bioinformatics), 10361 LNCS. https://doi.org/10.1007/978-3-319-63309-1_35

Yang, Y., Zoltan K., & Toth, C.K. (2017). Stereo image point cloud and Lidar point cloud fusion for the 3D street mapping. In *Annual Conference of the American Society of Photogrammtery and Remote Sensing (IGTF 2017–Imaging & Geospatial Technology Forum 2017), Baltimore, Maryland, March*, pp. 11–17.

5

Georeferencing 3D Models

5.1 Introduction

Geospatial engineers are well versed in dealing with spatial coordinate reference systems, whether in cadastres, land surveying, or engineering surveying. Architects and civil engineers can easily carry out three-dimensional calculations using local building coordinate systems. Problems with georeferencing arise on a practical level, especially when data are exchanged between these specialist areas. In the worst-case scenario, this exchange takes place without knowledge of relevant specific requirements or mathematical methods. In the best-case scenario, however, the exchange takes place with a comprehensive understanding of all transformation parameters at the mathematical, pragmatic, and data exchange levels.

5.1.1 Relevance and Use Cases

Georeferencing is an important prerequisite for successful BIM/GIS interoperability in all phases of building life cycles.

In the design and planning phase, the joint visualisation of building models and associated geospatial data is of crucial importance. In a BIM to GIS conversion, building models can be used for spatial analysis, such as for building permit procedures, traffic simulations, or environmental analysis. In GIS to BIM scenarios, the geographic contexts of building designs (i.e., alignment to property boundaries, terrain and ground, and placement of building polygons) can be used in BIM authoring tools.

Georeferencing is also required during the construction phase, e.g., for setting out machine guidance with high accuracy requirements, construction monitoring (e.g., with georeferenced point clouds), and area management on construction sites (storage area).

Georeferencing also plays an important role in the operation and maintenance phase of buildings. Use cases include seamless indoor–outdoor navigation and asset management. Both tasks require the use of a common

DOI: 10.1201/9781351200950-5

coordinate system. In indoor–outdoor navigation, a common coordinate system is required for the correct handling of positioning devices during navigation, while in facility management, all objects within facilities must be correctly located (georeferenced).

Coordinates are used to describe points in space. Coordinate systems describe the mathematical rules of how these coordinates are assigned to points. Coordinate reference systems are also firmly connected to real objects (e.g., the Earth or a building). The specifications of connections between the Earth and coordinate reference systems are called geodetic datum.

In BIM projects, building data and geospatial data, often with different coordinate reference systems, must be used together. Official geospatial data from public geospatial data infrastructure, specialist geospatial data, and topographic surveys are typically stored in superregional, distorted (because they are projected, i.e., separated by horizontal position and vertical height), or geodetic (i.e., Earth-related) coordinate reference systems. In building construction, on the other hand, 3D building models are almost always created in local, distortion-free (because they are Cartesian), and object-related (i.e., building-related) coordinate reference systems. If object-specific coordinate reference systems from BIM are related to higher-level geodetic coordinate reference systems by means of geometric transformation, this is referred to as georeferencing. Systematic deviations can occur during this transformation. The extent of these deviations depends on the following factors:

- The selected coordinate reference system;
- The length and height of the structure; and
- The location and elevation (NN//NHN altitude) of the BIM project.

Depending on the accuracy requirements and use case, any resulting deviations must be assessed to establish whether they can be neglected. For this reason, in addition to the choice of project coordinate system, transformation into higher-level coordinate reference systems, i.e., georeferencing, must be considered right at the start of construction projects.

5.1.2 State of the Art in Research and Technology

Georeferencing is used to give model coordinates Earth references. These coordinates, therefore, do not refer to an arbitrary coordinate system but are assigned to Earth-fixed geodetic datum. The GIS standard for georeferencing is given by International Standard Organization, 2019. ISO 19111 specifies all essential concepts and terms for geodetic, vertical, or local coordinate reference systems, different ways of defining geodetic datum, and the handling of Cartesian, ellipsoidal, polar, linear, and other coordinate systems. When transitioning between different coordinate reference systems, ISO 19111 distinguishes between the term "datum transformation" (i.e., transition from one datum to another) and "coordinate conversion" (i.e., retaining the datum). It is crucial for practical work that geodetic coordinate reference systems can be physically realised in reality, for example, with marked survey points. For the standardised and computer-interpretable representation as well-known text (WKT) of coordinate reference systems, the is ISO standard 19162 (ISO, 2019b) used by GIS software. A comprehensive description of all coordinate reference systems used worldwide is provided in the compendium *Geomatics Guidance Note, Coordinate Conversions and Transformations including Formulas* (International Association of Oil & Gas Producers, 2019), which is very suitable as a reference work, for example, for software development. These well-developed standards must be used as guidelines for all future developments regarding the georeferencing of BIM models.

In addition to the ISO standards, the topic of georeferencing has been discussed in numerous professional and scientific publications, especially concerning infrastructure data management in BIM and GIS.

The basic problem is that BIM software and collaboration platforms work exclusively with rectangular, Cartesian coordinate systems (Jaud et al., 2022). Therefore, the curvature of the Earth is not considered in these types of software or the associated exchange formats. Based on these geodetic principles, Jaud et al., 2020 stated that methods used in engineering geodesy significantly impact BIM workflows, especially when coordinate reference systems are used for elongated facilities in civil engineering and transport infrastructure. The basic problem is the conceptual discrepancy between the Cartesian, three-dimensional coordinate systems used for building models (CAD/BIM) and the coordinate reference systems of geodesy used in GIS, which are composed of projected horizontal positions and vertical (gravity-related) heights.

Jaud et al.'s (2020) exemplary calculations showed that this discrepancy also affects quantities derived from geometry, such as lengths and volumes. The aim of these approaches is always to create geodetic coordinate reference systems that can be transformed into other coordinate reference systems and minimise systematic deviations between curved-Earth and flat-Earth BIM.

Numerous methods for establishing local CRSs can be found in the scientific and technical literature, all of which aim to minimise local distortions caused by the Earth's curvature. Dennis (2015) showed the effects of different projection types in the context of low-distortion map projections. Other authors, e.g., (Baselga, 2021), have developed complex methods for high-elevation areas by adapting the ellipsoid dimension (a, b) for local measurements. An overview of the different concepts of ellipsoid fitting is given in Rollins & Meyer (2019). Important arguments for considering height in CRSs have been described in older studies by Burkholder (2004) regarding required height accuracy when determining the scale factor k_0.

FIGURE 5.1
LoGeoRef, the simple metric for the IFC concepts of georeferencing, can be used in information ordering to coordinate partial and specialised models of structures in infrastructure data management.

A practical approach is being taken, for example, in constructing the Brenner Base Tunnel (BBT) (Windischer et al., 2019). The centre meridian of a map projection (transversal Mercator) is adjusted so that the new coordinate reference system BBT_TM-WGS84 has no relevant scale in the project area and the coordinates can, therefore, be used directly and also in BIM software.

The approach of specifically adapting the transformation parameters of BIM projections was first implemented in Germany for the Hannover main station (Manthe & Clemen, 2015). This approach formed the basis for low-distortion projection as described in Clemen, Romanschek & Fleischer (2023) and later in this chapter.

When it comes to openBIM projects, the IFC standards were not clear with regard to georeferencing until version IFC4. The many IFC variants of georeferencing make the exchange of building models between BIM and GIS considerably more difficult. The LoGeoRef classification of the levels of georeferencing (Clemen & Görne, 2019), which are also identified by the ISO/TR 23262 (2021), specifies five possible levels (LoGeoRef 10, 20, 30, 40, and 50) in IFC files. The higher the level, the better the georeferencing is conceptually modelled. The levels do not refer to the quality (i.e., correctness and accuracy) of transformation parameters but refer to the IFC concepts used.

Therefore, it is not enough to require georeferencing with the current standards for information management: The IFC concept to be used must also be specified. If models are only to be annotated with simple metadata on geographical coordinates (i.e., longitude, latitude, and elevation), level 20 is sufficient, while LoGeoRef 50 (IfcMapConversion with IfcProjectedCRS) should be used for exact and uniform coordination. Levels 30 and 40 are only necessary if the target software used does not fully implement the IFC standards.

The interaction between geodesy, surveying, geoinformation, and BIM depends on many other factors in addition to georeferencing. Comprehensive overviews are provided by, for example, Herle et al. (2020) and Blankenbach et al. (2022).

TABLE 5.1

Description and comments on LoGeoRef according to Clemen & Görne (2019)

LoGeoRef	Description	Remark
0	No georeferencing	In the LoGeoRef metric, the information requirement "no georeferencing" must be explicitly specified.
10	Simple referencing via address information for a property (IfcSite) and/or building (IfcBuilding).	Additional information, not sufficient for georeferencing.
20	Simple point referencing via the geographical coordinates of a property (IfcSite).	Additional metadata, not sufficient for georeferencing.
30	Definition of a coordinate system for a property (IfcSite) or building (IfcBuilding) without relative reference to the other (higher-level) system. Level 30 is the current standard edition of BIM authoring software.	Sufficient for georeferencing but do not mix with LoGeoRef 40 or 50!
40	Definition of a project coordinate system (attribute: WorldCoordinateSystem) and specification of true north (as a direction vector of geographic north or grid north in the local coordinate system).	Sufficient for georeferencing but do not mix with LoGeoRef 30 or 50!
50	Specifications of offset and horizontal rotation for coordinate conversions between a project system and coordinate reference system (CRS). A CRS can be defined via an EPSG code, for example. This variant is only possible in the new IFC4 standard.	Standard for georeferencing but do not mix with LoGeoRef 30 or 40!

5.1.3 A Phenomenology of Georeferencing

The problem with georeferencing for BIM methods is complex. Different perspectives are described in the following phenomenology according to Jaud et al. (2022), briefly summarised in three levels:

1. The a priori level is independent of BIM and includes given mathematical and geodetic concepts, such as coordinate systems,

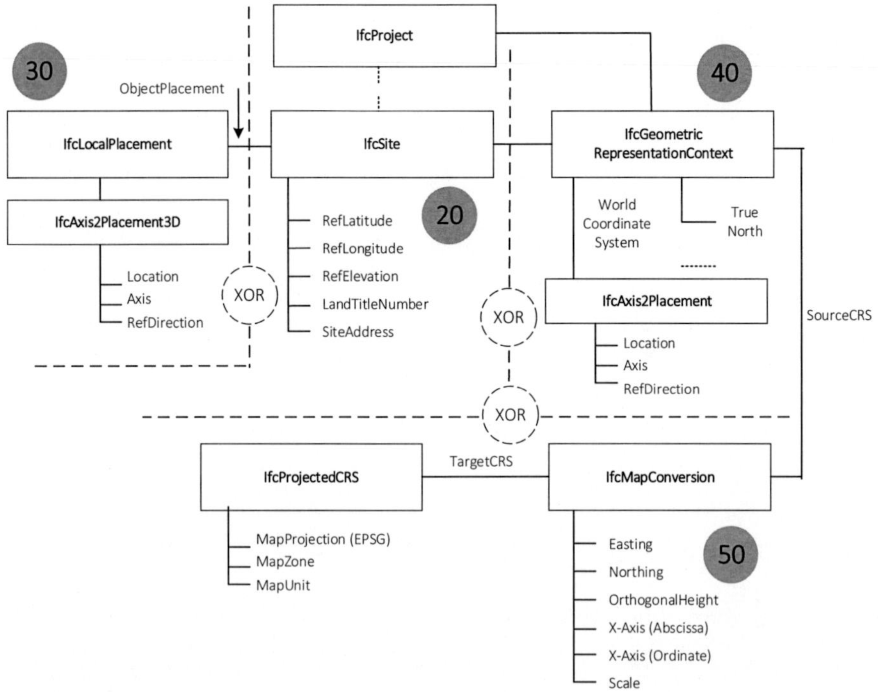

FIGURE 5.2
IFC concepts for georeferencing. While level 20 may be interpreted as metadata with geographic coordinates, IFC models should use either level 30 (IfcSite), 40 (IfcGeometricRepresentationContext), or 50 (IfcMapConversion).

conversion methods, reference bodies (e.g., ellipsoids), cartographic projections, geodetic datum, coordinate transformation, coordinate reference systems (e.g., the European Terrestrial Reference System 1989 (ETRS89) and Universal Transverse Mercator projection (UTM)), and geometric–physical concepts for elevation models (e.g., geoid, etc.);

2. The possibility level includes the methodological requirements of specialist domains (such as OGC/ISO standards, e.g., ISO 19111, ISO 19148, WKT ISO 19162, EPSG codes, and ISO 19650), interfaces for the exchange between BIM and GIS software (e.g., IFC, GML, native formats, etc.), and functionalities of the software (e.g., is georeferencing conceptualised/correctly implemented/parameterisable in the software?);
3. At the pragmatic level, the focus is on implementation in actual projects, including geospatial awareness in project management, specialist knowledge and mutual understanding between participants,

guidelines for quality assurance (e.g., information exchange requirements, checking tools, etc.), and practical skills in the operation of software for modelling and collaboration.

5.2 Reasons for Systematic Deviations

Regarding the "the planning and construction with state plane coordinates", Heunecke (2017) described the necessary reduction formulas for the project scale m_P based on UTM map projection and project height, as well as problematising changes Δ m_P in project scale and the non-parallelism of the Z-directions. The implementation of these engineering geodetic methods in BIM software should be considered as early as possible, i.e., in early planning phases, so that no systematic deviations occur during the construction phase.

The causes of deviations between geodetic position reference systems for surveying and three-dimensional, Cartesian coordinates for (local) building models are summarised below. A detailed description can be found, for example, in building SMART Australasia (2020).

5.2.1 Height Correction

As position coordinates are calculated on reference ellipsoids, the elevation of construction sites must be considered. Due to the divergence of plumb lines (Figure 5.3), the actual distance between two points increases with the height above the reference ellipsoid. Measured horizontal distances must, therefore, be reduced during the transition from reality to (position) coordinate reference systems. This height correction amounts to up to -16 cm/km at normal heights of up to 1000 m during the transition from reality to the formula $dist'_H = dist_H * (1 - h_{mean}/R)$, where h is the mean height above the ellipsoid and R is the mean radius of curvature (approx. 6381 km). When calculating height correction, height anomalies (i.e., the difference between geoids and reference ellipsoids) must also be considered.

5.2.2 Mapping Correction

In geodesy, map projections (Figure 5.4) convert geographical or ellipsoidal coordinates (Φ, Λ) into Cartesian coordinates (x, y). Curved surfaces, such as those of rotational ellipsoids, cannot be mapped onto flat surfaces without the occurrence of distortions. To use geodetic reference systems for rotational ellipsoids with conformal mappings, Universal Transverse Mercator coordinates (UTM; scale = 0.9996) and transversal Mercator coordinates

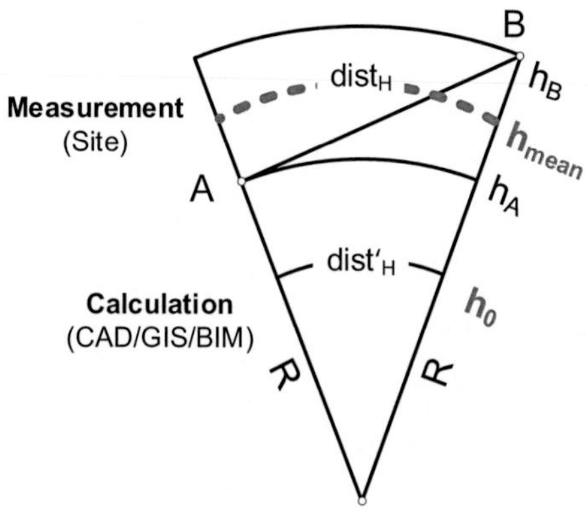

FIGURE 5.3
Horizontal distances measured on construction sites must be projected into the calculation plane due to the height. (Clemen, Romanschek & Fleischer, 2023.)

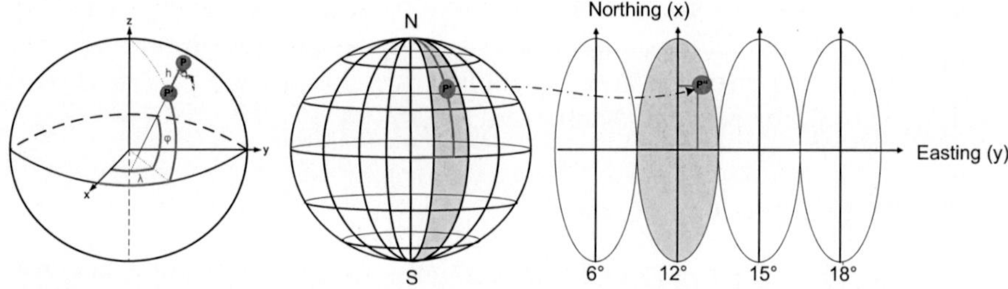

FIGURE 5.4
Cartographic mapping describing the functional mapping of ellipsoidal coordinates (left) to levelled/projected coordinates (e.g., UTM). Geodetic datum (e.g., ETRS89) do not change during projection. (Clemen, Romanschek & Fleischer, 2023.)

(TM; e.g., with scale = 1), for example, are used, in which maps are isogonal but have unavoidable variations in the scales of distances and areas. These distortions must be applied as corrections when transferring actual (natural) distances into projected distances (e.g., maps and GIS).

5.2.3 Earth Curvature Reduction

Earth curvature reduction is assumed to be the difference between the actual curved line of the same height and the length of the line in a tangential plane. For distances up to 10 km, however, this horizontal difference is no more than 1 mm and can usually be neglected in practice (Witte et al., 2020).

5.2.4 Total Reduction of Measured Horizontal Distances

Total reduction is the sum of all correction values, including the following:

- Map correction due to the projection of curved surfaces onto a plane;
- Height correction due to the divergence of plumb lines from height; and
- Correction of the Earth's curvature (which can generally be neglected),

whereby the corrections can accumulate or partially cancel each other out.

An example from *The Guidelines for Geodesy and BIM* (DVW e.V. & Runder Tisch GIS e.V., 2022) shows the highest point in North Rhine-Westphalia, i.e., the Langenberg, near the central meridian (ETRS89/UTM coordinates: E = 32469200.000, N = 5680660.000 at an elevation of 843 m above sea level), with a mapping reduction of -40 cm/km and an elevation reduction of -14 cm/km, resulting in a combined reduction of -54 cm/km and thus, a project scale of 0.999460 from reality into the ETRS89/UTM coordinate reference system.

These corrections must be made at the transition between both surveying/GIS and realty (i.e., as-built documentation, staking out, etc.) and surveying/GIS and scale-free CAD/BIM models.

5.2.5 "True North" and Meridian Convergence

The north problem occurs when the transformation of federated 3D models is carried out improperly, namely only as translations. The meridian convergence is incorrectly ignored if models from different coordinate reference systems are only shifted to the correct position. Therefore, geospatial experts should always carry out transformations, including meridian convergence, between different coordinate reference systems.

5.2.6 Large Coordinates and Parametric Solid Models

Small deviations in georeferencing can also occur in the calculation kernels of CAD/BIM software. As a rule, 3D CAD software cannot handle large coordinates. Errors can also commonly be caused in coordinate transformations due to the fact that parametric solid models can only be transferred to other coordinate reference systems with great effort because they may involve non-linear transformations.

The usual transformations, according to the BIM method (see Section 4 of this chapter), only apply to localised areas of 100 m to 5 km. Elongated systems (e.g., roads, railways, and waterways) may have to be broken down into subsections. Transition zones must be defined between these subsections. For this purpose, Jaud et al. (2020) recommend, among other things, the uniform approximation of project scales between the spatially separated subsections, limited to transition zones.

5.3 Types of Georeferencing 3D BIM Models

This section describes the types of georeferencing 3D BIM models used at a high abstraction level. This section does not offer recommendations but rather provides a framework for understanding georeferencing using illustrative concepts instead of mathematical terms. Mathematical parameterisation is explained in Section 5.2.

5.3.1 Not Georeferenced

Model coordinate systems (MCSs) are not related to any coordinate reference systems (CRSs); only local three-dimensional coordinates are used (Figure 5.5). This type can be used if no geospatial data are to be added to

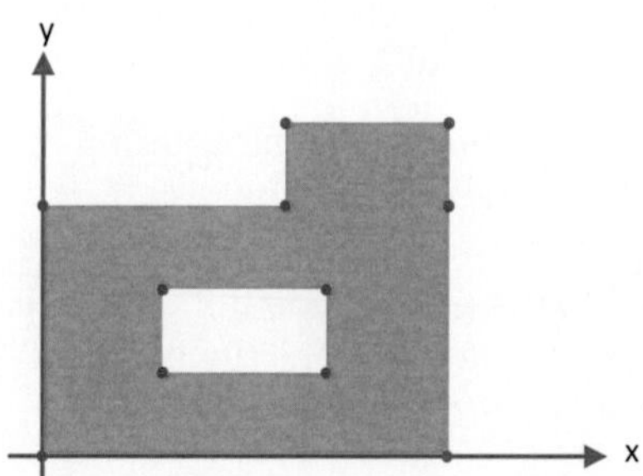

FIGURE 5.5
A (red) model coordinate system (MCS) that is not georeferenced.

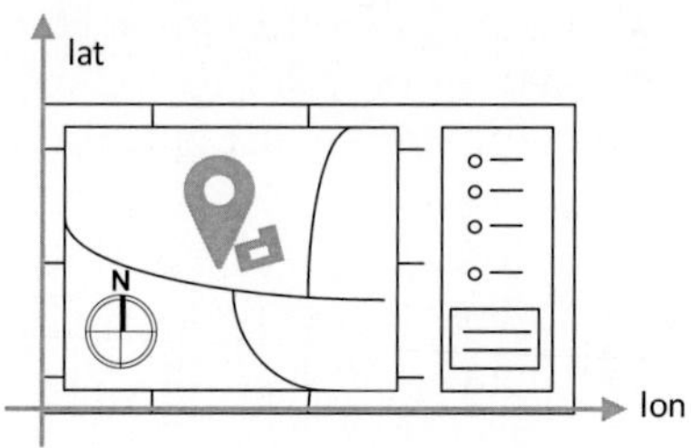

FIGURE 5.6
BIM that is approximately placed on a map using geographic coordinates as metadata.

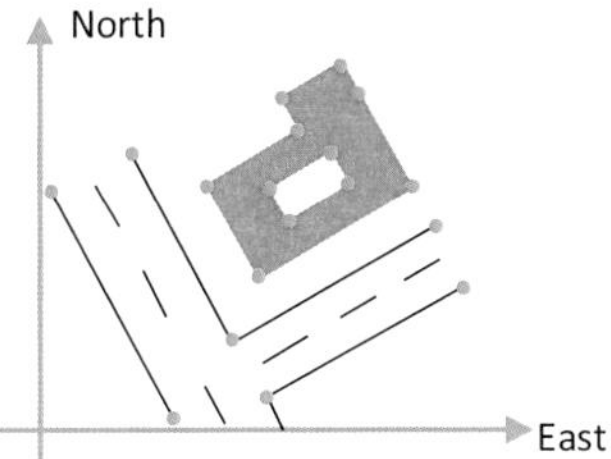

FIGURE 5.7
An entire BIM project using direct positioning in a projected CRS (e.g., an infrastructure project).

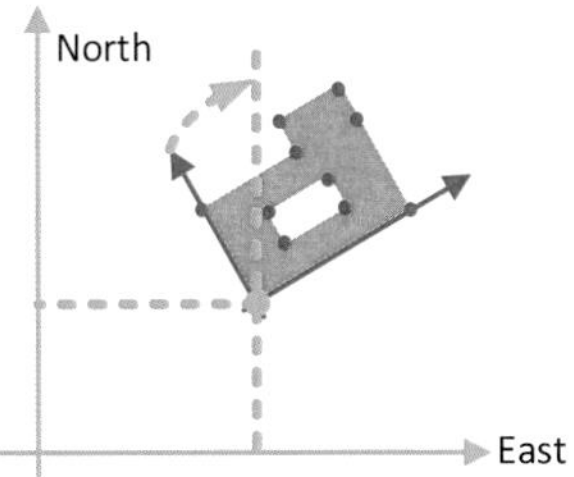

FIGURE 5.8
A (red) model coordinate system (MCS) that is horizontally positioned in a (green) projected CRS, specifying easting, northing, height, and the north direction in the building reference points.

BIM projects, no topographic surveys are needed, and the as-built models are not to be later integrated into 3D GIS or asset management systems.

5.3.2 Georeferenced by Geographic Coordinates

Model coordinate systems (MCSs) are attached to metadata regarding latitude, longitude, and elevation, e.g., the geographic reference system WGS84 (Figure 5.6). This type can be used if models are to be represented as points on a map or in a GIS.

5.3.3 Georeferenced by Geodetic Coordinates

Model coordinate systems (MCSs) are equivalent to coordinate reference systems (CRSs) used in surveying/GIS (Figure 5.7). The locations of all objects are directly given in (map-) projected CRS. This type can be used if large-scale or extended planning is carried out exclusively in GIS or special CAD software for infrastructure.

5.3.4 Georeferenced by Project Base Points and Orientations

The location of models with respect to surveying systems is given by the base points' easting, northing, north orientation, and elevation in coordinate reference systems (CRSs, Figure 5.8). CRSs may include (flat-Earth approximation) engineering CRS or geodetic/projected CRS. This level can be used when MCS models and other built-environment models need to be transformed into common coordinate reference systems (CRSs) in order to be usable in conjunction with geospatial information and surveys.

Coordinate reference systems (CRSs) can be specified in natural language, as EPSG codes, or as computer-interpretable well-known text (WKT; ISO 19162).

5.3.5 Georeferenced by Intermediate CRS for BIM Projects

Subordinate project coordinate systems can be agreed upon if BIM projects have several buildings or constructions (models) in multiple locations. Multiple BIM systems (MCSs, e.g., the system shown in red in Figure 5.9) are then specified relative to project coordinate systems (PCSs, e.g., the system shown in blue in Figure 5.9), while those PCSs are specified relative to coordinate reference systems (CRSs, e.g., the system shown in green in Figure 5.9).

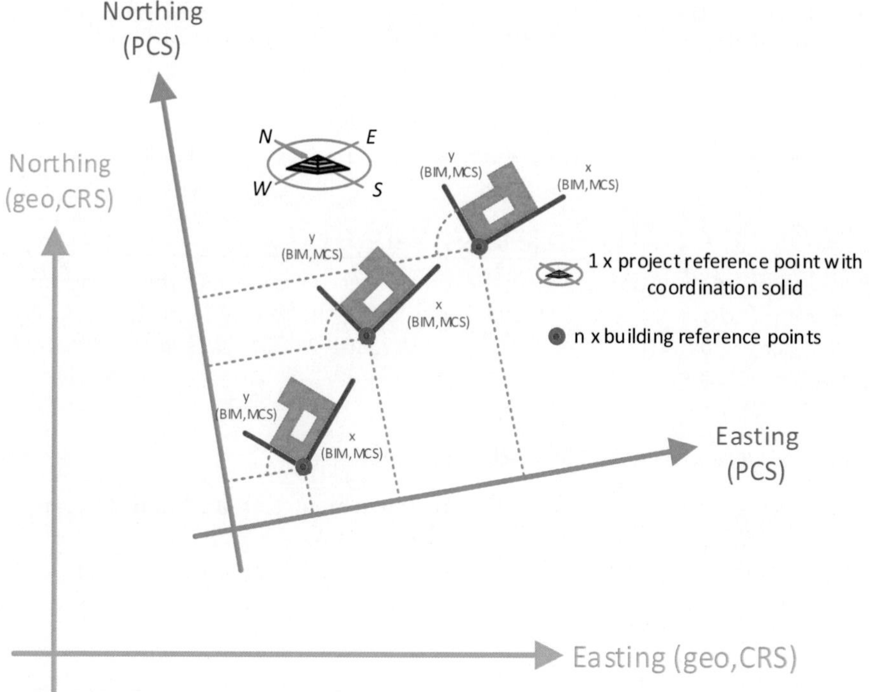

FIGURE 5.9
A low-distortion projected (LDP) CRS (blue) intermediating regional CRS (green) in GIS and local Cartesian BIM systems (red).

5.3.6 Additional Elements for Georeferencing

Solid placeholders (coordination bodies), representing commonly agreed surveying points, may also be required. These virtual objects have to be positioned in every model in order to visually validate the correct position when combining federated models in common coordination models. Solid placeholders have the same CRS coordinates in all federated models but may have different coordinate values in model coordinate systems (MCSs).

To realise coordinate systems, surveying points (e.g., benchmarks and ground control points) are marked in the relevant localities. In BIM projects, these points may need to be virtually modelled as 3D objects (Figure 5.10).

5.4 Types of Transformation

The most important transformation parameters are as follows:

- X_0 = Easting of building reference points in geodetic CRSs;
- Y_0 = Northing of building reference points in geodetic CRSs;
- α = The north direction, rotated around the z-axis and measured in relation to building reference points;
- S_P = Project scale, based on cartographic projection and height above ellipsoids;
- H_0 = Geodetic height of project base points.

The neglection, combination, and order of application of these parameters imply a diverse range of transformation types for BIM projects, which this section will discuss (Figure 5.12).

It should also be noted whether these transformation parameters refer to entire BIM projects (e.g., districts, construction sites, factory sites, etc.) or single structures (e.g., buildings, bridges, road sections, etc.) to a limited extent.

To simplify matters, compound coordinate reference systems (CRSs), which distinguish between position and height, are referred to below as "2D+1D", while geocentric Cartesian coordinate systems are labelled "3D".

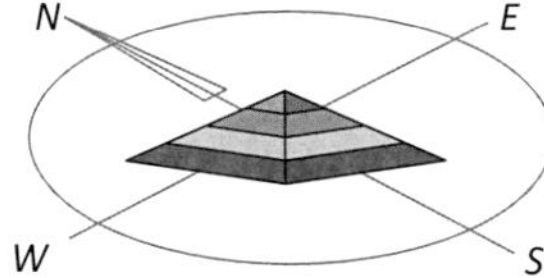

FIGURE 5.10
A coordination solid. As part of BIM, coordination solids help to check the georeferencing of federated models.

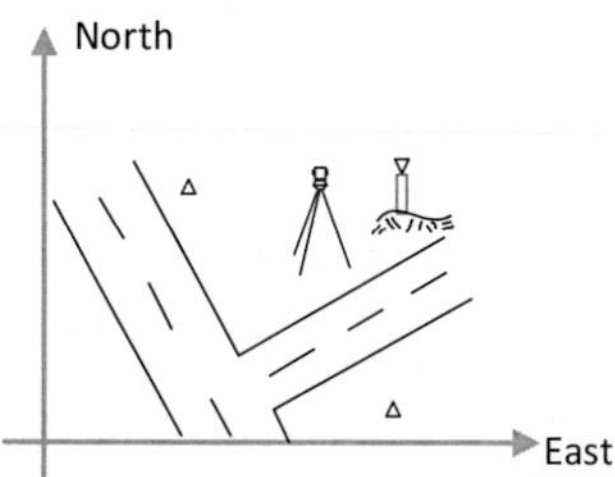

FIGURE 5.11
The permanent storage of benchmarks as part of virtual BIM models helps to coordinate surveying tasks and provide a deeper understanding of georeferencing.

V1: Surveying/GIS and BIM with identical coordinate systems.

In V1, both domains use identical coordinate systems. This happens in the infrastructure sector, for example, when BIM planning is only carried out in official, georeferenced coordinate reference systems (V1a). Or, as in monument preservation, for example, surveying is carried out directly in building coordinate systems (V1b). Some research projects, e.g., Wunderlich (2021), use Earth-centred and Earth-fixed (ECEF) Cartesian 3D coordinate reference systems (V1c) together. The advantage of this approach is scale-free georeferencing, but this comes at the cost of using much less intuitively usable coordinate systems or less descriptive coordinate values.

V2: Transformation parameters (2D+1D) between surveying/GIS and BIM.

V2a, 2b, and 2c each refer to transformation between official surveying/GIS and building coordinate systems. The transformation parameters for the positions of building reference points (X_0, Y_0, and H_0) in coordinate reference systems are defined and applied uniformly in these BIM projects. The north direction α, which is the angle between the geodetic grid north and the y-axis of the building system, is also defined. However, all software systems involved must apply the north rotation correctly. BIM software sometimes converts the direction of rotation incorrectly due to the orientation (left vs. right system) and direction of rotation (clockwise vs. counterclockwise). The effect of the project scale S_P can be problematic because scales are not applied in typical building construction BIM software during transformations. The questions, therefore, arise as to how large these relative deviations between surveying/GIS and BIM are and whether they are tolerable. These questions must be answered separately for each BIM project because the project scale S_P depends on the type of projection (e.g., GK, UTM, etc.), the geographical location of the building (i.e., distance from the central meridian), and the height of the terrain. Based on these prior investigations, decisions can be made whether to implement transformations by neglecting the

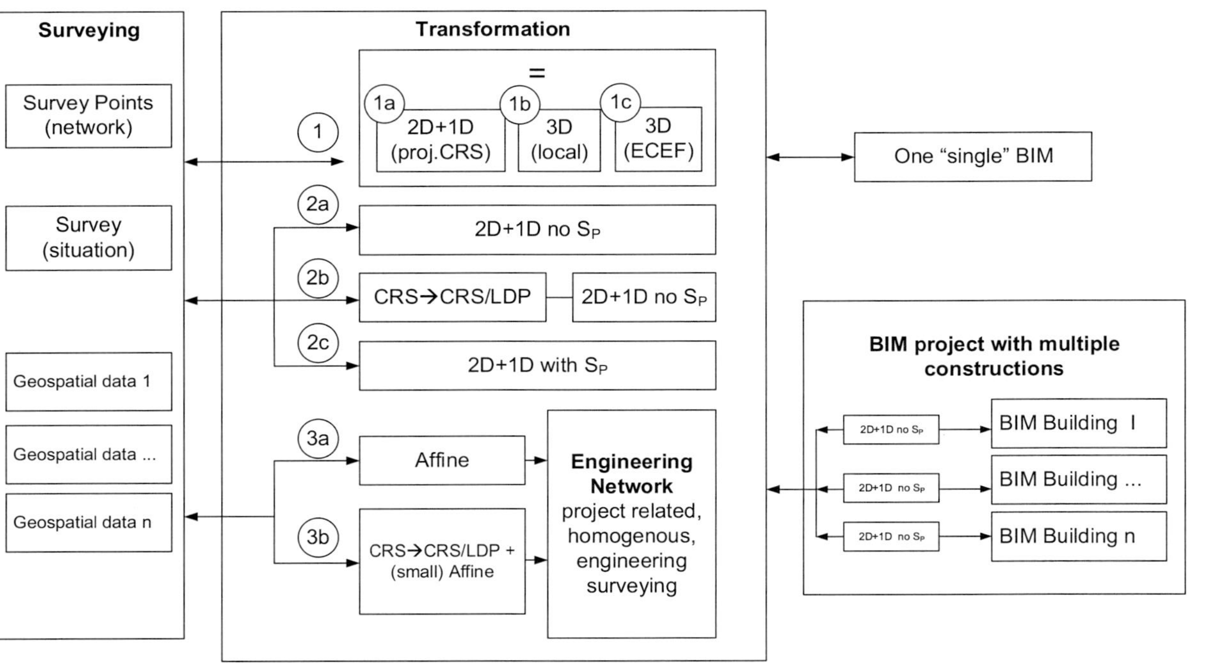

FIGURE 5.12
Overview of the variants presented (V1, V2, and V3) for pragmatic approaches for the georeferencing of BIM models. (Clemen et al., 2022.)

scale S_P (V2a), add intermediates that perform low-distortion projection (LDP) on the same geodetic datum (V2b), or apply the scale S_P in CAD/BIM software (V2c), which is rarely supported by CAD/BIM software.

V3: Double transformation between GIS, surveying/special networks, and BIM.

In order to transfer scale-free BIM planning to reality without geometric tensions, special, homogeneous engineering survey networks with the highest precision must be established onsite. Single BIM models or multiple BIM models can only be placed in local coordinate systems via rigid transformations (X_0, Y_0, α, and H_0). However, precise engineering networks need to be georeferenced with affine transformations (V3a) or a combination of low-distortion projection (LDP) and small affine corrections (V3b).

5.5 Low-Distortion Projection (LDP): Example German Railway (DB)

The barrier-free renovation of 5400 passenger stations in the German railway system (Deutsche Bahn, DB) has been supported by BIM since 2017. BIM focuses on three-dimensional planning and model coordination; however, 3D software solutions do not work with geodetic coordinates, which causes systematic deviations. In local projects, such as the planning of engineering structures or passenger stations, the use of Cartesian coordinates is essential as these form the basis of planning software for architects and civil, electrical, and mechanical engineers. The solution is to convert geodetic coordinates into optimised coordinate reference systems. This procedure was standardised and implemented for all 5400 traffic stations to avoid systematic deviations (see Section 5.2) and used DB_REF geodetic datum for alignment references. This enabled the precise use of geometric information, facilitated the transfer to other coordinate systems, and supported the direct staking out of construction projects from the model.

In *The Guide to Geodesy and BIM*, Reifenhäuser & Wunderlich (2022) explained the specific BIM requirements for using the DB_REF coordinate reference system in railroad infrastructure. The authors advocated a "uniform approach that ensures the homogeneous and true-to-scale integration of all BIM models". They emphasised that alignment must be carried out according to cartographic mapping, even when using the BIM method, due to the requirements of the regulations. In 3D BIM for local planning, such as engineering structures, alignment can be converted into 3D space curves. Local Cartesian coordinate systems are created using control points, with the z-axis approximating the perpendicular direction.

The challenge for German railway project was combining the geodetic perspective for qualified alignment in high-speed train construction (DB_REF; GIS) with the Cartesian perspective of local construction planning (3D; CAD systems). The solution lay in the cartographic conversion (not datum transformation!) of the geodetic coordinates to minimise systematic deviations between the 3D planning and surveying through the optimal definition of a coordinate reference system (CRS). Low-distortion projections (LDP) were also inserted for each passenger station in the railway system.

Using this new uniform and standardised procedure, a local CRS was created for all 5400 stations and made available as a database on the info platform. This type of CRS is called a local coordinate system for passenger stations (VA system for short). The conversion of local VA systems into DB_REF is easy to implement using GIS and CAD software and is based on common IT standards, namely WKT/CRS (ISO, 2019b). VA systems and DB_REF/GK differ only slightly: Instead of a global Gauss–Krüger (equals a transversal Mercator with a scale of 1) mapping with 3° meridian strips, VA systems use locally optimised cartographic projections for each station, which minimises systematic deviations to a maximum of 2 ppm (or 2mm/1km).

The local coordinate system for the passenger stations in Germany used the uniform geodetic datum DB_REF as a basis, which guarantees alignment references. The high network quality (absolute value of 1 cm all over Germany/relative value of 5 mm) of DB_REF was retained in the passenger station coordinate system.

With this new standardised procedure, geometric information can continue to be used in the correct position, even in the years after planning, and can be transferred and integrated into other CRSs; the geodetic datum remain

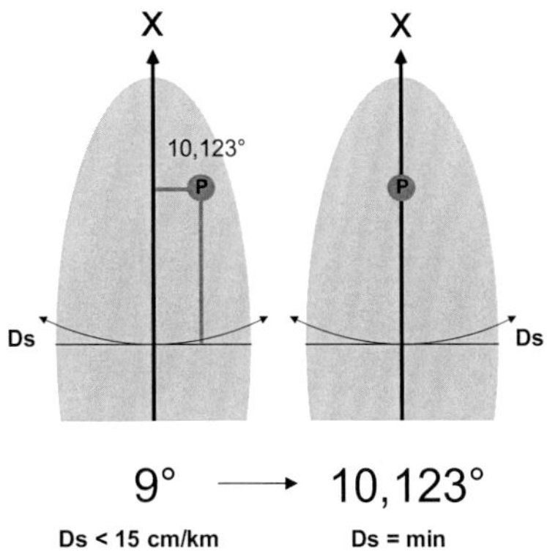

FIGURE 5.13
Instead of integer transversal Mercator (TM) centre meridians (3°, 6°, 9°, 12°…), VA systems use TM projection through the ellipsoidal coordinates of traffic facilities (VA) (Clemen, Romanschek & Fleischer, 2023) in the same geodetic datum (DB_REF).

unchanged and, in contrast to the Helmert and Affine transformations via identical points, no heuristic assumptions are introduced. The parameters in the created VA system databases parameterise the automated transformation of DB_REF coordinates to local systems and back. In the German example, the parameters (i.e., the values of the VA system database) were calculated under the following premises:

- The parameters described a compound 2D+1D coordinate reference system (CRS) consisting of position and height;
- The geodetic datum of the DB_REF (position and ellipsoid dimensions) remained unchanged and no geodetic datum transformations took place;
- Only (cartographic) projections were adjusted. The centre meridian λ_0 of transversal Mercator projections ran through the given geographical coordinates of the railway stations;
- The origins of the projections were defined by latitude and longitude (φ_0,λ_0). The local VA system coordinates were given a supplement in the east direction (f_E = 5000 m) and north direction (f_N = 10,000 m) to avoid negative coordinate values in the BIM models;
- The scale k_0 of the Mercator projections was optimised so that the difference between the measured horizontal distances and the distances calculated from the coordinates in the projection plane was minimised locally. The exclusive influencing factor for k_0 was the height of the project areas and the quasigeoid deviation was considered;
- The heights in the VA system were identical to those in DB_REF2016 (same vertical data);
- A zip-folder was created for each VA system, which contained the parameters according to ISO 19162 (i.e., well-known text representations of coordinate reference systems) in the syntactic dialects of SIMPLE, SFSQL, GDAL, ESRI, ProjJSON, GML, and a special Autodesk xml format, among others.

With these parameters, the goal of minimising systematic deviations between surveying and 3D software was achieved. If survey models (i.e., fixed points, topographical surveys, 3D point clouds, etc.) are available in VA systems, they can be used directly by 3D BIM software. To put it bluntly, the Earth can remain a disc for BIM.

In order to minimise systematic deviations between surveying and 3D modelling, DB_REF coordinates are converted into VA system coordinates after network densification but before construction project-related surveying in the relevant areas. In the German example, the following processes were utilised (Figure 5.14):

1. Densification of the DB_REF Survey Network.

   Network densification was carried out in accordance with all quality specifications and procedural regulations of the German railway network and the points were marketed and documented onsite.

2. Conversion from DB_REF to VA System.

   The fixed points were automatically transferred to the VA system of the railway stations. For this purpose, the VA system database provided the parameters for all passenger stations.

3. Project-Related Densification of the Survey Network.

   Network consolidation was carried out according to geodetic engineering requirements in the scale-free VA system and the points were marketed and documented onsite.

4. Measuring Object Points and 3D Laser Scanning.

   The point clouds and coordinates of the object points were measured and registered in the VA system (measured points form the basis of 3D modelling in CAD, GIS, and BIM and there are no systematic differences between surveying and modelling in 3D software). The influence of the Earth's curvature on the position coordinates could be neglected due to the transformations.

5. Scale-Free and Homogeneous 3D Modelling.

   All dimensions and quantities could be derived from the 3D models without a correction factor.

Complete toolboxes for implementing VA systems in projects, including the databases (in this case, the definition files for the 5400 stations), can be found on information platforms for construction, systems engineering, and

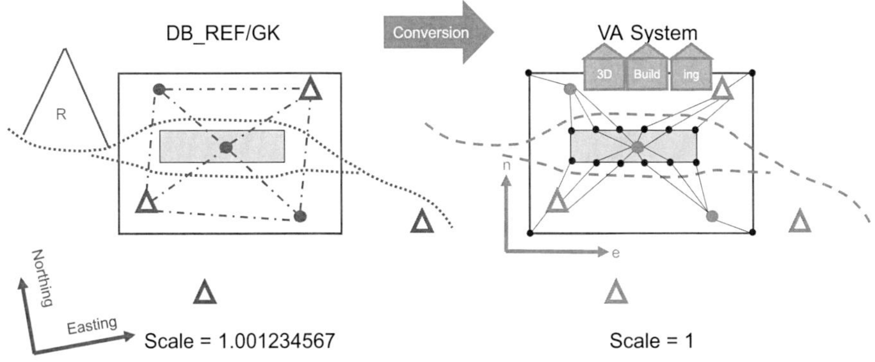

FIGURE 5.14
Higher-level network densification and alignment taking place in the global CRS DB_REF, demonstrating local densification, object measurement, and modelling in a VA system.

IT/TC for passenger stations, which are freely accessible on the internet. In the German example, the VA system database had a separate folder for each station number, which contained the small definition files. In addition to the ISO 19162:2019 standard, WKT dialects for ESRI and a special format for Autodesk and Bentley products were also provided. The appropriate WKT file could be integrated with just a few clicks or standard commands in the GIS or CAD system. The software was then able to use the VA system together with DB_REF/GK or the coordinate reference system for the national survey.

5.6 Summary

Georeferencing 3D building models can be achieved when all parties understand the properties of coordinate reference systems, agree on suitable transformation parameters for BIM projects, and correctly implement transformations in the data formats and software used. Precise georeferencing is necessary for integrating 3D building models and geospatial data. In the next chapter, we will discuss BIM and GIS integration beyond georeferencing.

Acknowledgements

Individual text excerpts from this article were published by the authors in German in Clemen et al. (2022), Clemen, Romanschek & Fleischer (2023), and Clemen, Gruner & Pfeifer (2023) and were based on professional collaboration with the respective co-authors.

Bibliography

Baselga, S. (2021) "Two Conformal Projections for Constant-Height Surface to Plane Mapping", *Journal of Surveying Engineering*, Vol. 147, No. 2, S. 6020004.

Blankenbach, J., Clemen, C. & Becker, R. (2022) "Grundlagen und Informations Management der BIM-Methode", in DVW e.V. & Runder Tisch GIS e.V. (Hg.) *Leitfaden Geodäsie und BIM: Version 3.1* [Online], Bühl/München, S. 17–50. available under www.dvw.de/BIM-Leitfaden.pdf.

building SMART Australasia. (2020) "User Guide for Geo-referencing in IFC", Vol. 2 [Online]. available under www.buildingsmart.org / wp- content/ uploads/ 2020/ 02/ User- Guide- for- Geo- referencing- in- IFC- v2.0.pdf.

Burkholder, E. F. (2004) "Accuracy of Elevation Reduction Factor", *Journal of Surveying Engineering*, Vol. 130, No. 3, S. 134–137.

Clemen, C., Becker, R., Kaden, R. & Blankenbach, J. (2022) "Georeferenzierung", in DVW e.V. & Runder Tisch GIS e.V. (Ed.) *Leitfaden Geodäsie und BIM: Version 3.1* [Online], Bühl/München, S. 50–65. available under www.dvw.de/BIM-Leitfaden.pdf.

Clemen, C. & Görne, H. (2019) "Level of Georeferencing (LoGeoRef) using IFC for BIM", *Journal of Geodesy, Cartography and Cadastre*, Vol. 10, No. 3, S. 15–20 [Online]. available under www. jgcc.geoprevi.ro / docs/ 2019/ 10/ jgcc_ 2019_ no10_ 3.pdf (Abgerufen am 5 January 2024).

Clemen, C., Gruner, F. & Pfeifer, J. (2023) *Infrastrukturdatenhaltung mit BIM und GIS*. Forschungsbericht 46 (2023), Deutsches Zentrum für Schienenverkehrsforschung beim Eisenbahn-Bundesamt, Dresden, Germany http://doi.org/10.48755/dzsf.230015.01

Clemen, C., Romanschek, E. & Fleischer, A. (2023) "Georeferenzierung von 3D-Modellen mit dem VA-System für Personenbahnhöfe: Das neue „Koordinatensystem Personenbahnhöfe" minimiert systematische Abweichungen zwischen Vermessung und 3D-Planung.", in VDEI (Ed.) *Der Eisenbahningenieur* [Online], DVV Media Group / Eurailpress, S. 56–59. available under www.eurailpress-archiv.de/.

Dennis, M. L. (2015) "Ground Truth: Design and Documentation of Low Distortion Projections for Surveying and GIS", Professional Land Surveyors of Oregon 2015 Annual Conference, USA.

DVW e.V. & Runder Tisch GIS e.V. Ed. (2022) *Leitfaden Geodäsie und BIM: Version 3.1* [Online], Bühl/München. available under www.dvw.de/BIM- Leitfaden.pdf.

Herle, S., Becker, R., Wollenberg, R. & Blankenbach, J. (2020) "GIM and BIM", *PFG – Journal of Photogrammetry, Remote Sensing and Geoinformation Science*, Vol. 88, No. 1, S. 33–42.

Heunecke, O. (2017) "Planung und Umsetzung von Bauvorhaben mit amtlichen Lage- und Höhenkoordinaten", *zfv – Zeitschrift für Geodäsie, Geoinformation und Landmanagement*, Vol. 3/2017, S. 180–187.

International Association of Oil & Gas Producers (2019) *Coordinate Conversions and Transformations including Formulas: Geomatics Guidance Note Number 7, part 2* [Online] (373-7-2). available under www.iogp.org / bookstore/ product/ coordinate- conversions- and- transformation- including- formulas/ .

ISO (2019a) *ISO 19111 Geographic information — Referencing by coordinates*. International Organization for Standardization, Geneva, Switzerland. https://www.iso.org/standard/74039.html

ISO (2019b) *ISO 19162 Geographic information – Well-known text representation of coordinate reference systems*, Geneva, Switzerland. https://www.iso.org/standard/76496.html

ISO (2021) *ISO/TR 23262 Geographic information — GIS (geospatial) / BIM interoperability*. International Organization for Standardization, Geneva, Switzerland. www.iso.org/standard/75105.html

Jaud, Š., Clemen, C., Muhič, S. & Borrmann, A. (2022) "Georeferencing in IFC: Meeting the requirements of infrastructure and building industries", *ISPRS Annals of the Photogrammetry, Remote Sensing and Spatial Information Sciences*, Vol. X-4/W2-2022, S. 145–152.

Jaud, Š., Donaubauer, A., Heunecke, O. & Borrmann, A. (2020, October) "Georeferencing in the context of building information modelling", *Automation in Construction*, Vol. 118, 103211. https://doi.org/10.1016/j.autcon.2020.103211

Manthe, C. & Clemen, C. (2015) "TLS für das Building Information Modeling (BIM) – Das BIM-Pilotprojekt Erneuerung Hbf Hannover: Beiträge zum 147. DVW-Seminar am 7. und 8. Dezember 2015 in Fulda", *Terrestrisches Laserscanning 2015 (TLS 2015)*, No. 81 [Online]. available under www.geodaesie.info/sr/terrestrisches-laserscanning-2015-tls-20155182/1950.

Reifenhäuser, M. & Wunderlich, T. (2022) "Geodätischer Raumbezug der Eisenbahn-Infrastruktur +", in DVW e.V. & Runder Tisch GIS e.V. (Hg.) *Leitfaden Geodäsie und BIM: Version 3.1* [Online], Bühl/München, S. 179–181. available under www.dvw.de/BIM-Leitfaden.pdf.

Rollins, C. M. & Meyer, T. H. (2019) "Four Methods for Low-Distortion Projections", *Journal of Surveying Engineering*, Vol. 145, No. 4, S. 4019017.

Windischer, G., Hofmann, M., Glatzl, R. & Bergmeister, K. (2019) "Modellierung von Tunnelbauwerken in BIM-Systemen unter Berücksichtigung besonderer Referenzsysteme für den länderübergreifenden Lage- und Höhenbezug", *allgemeine vermessungs-nachrichten (avn)*, 6-7 [Online]. available under www.gispoint.de / artikelarchiv/ avn/ 2019/ avn- ausgabe- 6- 72019/ 5944- modellierung-von-tunnelbauwerken-in-bim-systemen-unter-beruecksichtigung-besonderer-referenzsysteme- fuer- den- laenderuebergreifenden- lage- und- hoehenbezug.html.

Witte, B., Sparla, P. & Blankenbach, J. (2020) *Vermessungskunde für das Bauwesen mit Grundlagen des Building Information Modeling (BIM) und der Statistik* [Online], Berlin, Offenbach, Wichmann. available under www.content-select.com / index.php? id= bib_view& ean= 9783879076581.

Wunderlich, T. (2021) "Misalignment—Can 3D BIM Overrule Professional Setting-out According to Plane and Height?", *Contributions to International Conferences on Engineering Surveying*, S. 3–12 [Online]. DOI: 10.1007/978-3-030-51953-7_1.

6

BIM and GIS Integration

6.1 Introduction

As discussed, BIM is a methodology for supporting the planning, construction, and operation of buildings through coordinated data management and the resulting improved use of information. This method is currently mainly used for the planning and construction of buildings but is also required in the infrastructure sector in many countries. It has been shown that BIM can be used to identify and solve problems in the early stages of the planning and construction processes. *The Guidelines for Major Projects*, published by the German Federal Ministry of Transport (BMDV)[1] in 2015, recommend digital planning methods under the motto "Plan first, then build", especially to ensure the "accuracy of fit" of specialist planning at the interfaces between domains. Higher planning costs resulting from the use of the BIM method are demonstrably offset by the advantages of better coordinated planning, which lead to lower costs in the construction phase (European Commission, 2021). In addition, the reliability and predictability of costs and deadlines increase significantly.

Geospatial data are data with spatial references and are particularly needed in the areas of construction planning and approval. Geospatial data can be recorded, managed, analysed, and graphically displayed in so-called GIS. Most geospatial data are two-dimensional. Typical examples include the following:

- Property and land information with the Geography Markup Language (GML) application schema, e.g., the national official cadastral information system;
- Environmental data (e.g., the European SDI "Infrastructure for Spatial Information in the European Community" (INSPIRE)); and
- Site plans for specific, event-driven, and local surveys.

Digital terrain models (DTMs) are referred to as 2.5-dimensional because they assign exactly one height to each horizontal position coordinate. On

DOI: 10.1201/9781351200950-6

the other hand, 3D city models depict the urban planning context using the CityGML application schema, for example.

The main differences between the use of BIM for the planning, construction, and operation of transportation facilities and its use for building construction are the spatial extents and alignment references of elongated facilities (Borrmann, 2022). Currently, available BIM tools/software are geared towards construction projects with limited extents but high precision. In contrast, geographic information systems consider large, often nationwide to global datasets that can contain information about the environment, as well as data on transportation and supply infrastructure systems.

From a practical point of view, the information models, interfaces, and tools for capturing, managing, analysing, and presenting should be usable between the system boundaries of BIM and GIS without obstacle. The following very general requirements for information systems are also identified for BIM/GIS interoperability by (Clemen et al., 2023):

- The data basis for decisions is reproducible;
- Relevant information is accessible, linked, and machine-interpretable;
- Information delivery can be automatically quality-assured;
- Each piece of information only needs to be entered once.

These goals can currently only be partially realised through BIM and GIS integration. For more than 15 years, very different solution approaches have been discussed scientifically, standardised by administration and industry, implemented by software manufacturers, developed in projects, and applied in business processes. The aim of this chapter is to identify and classify these different approaches, validate them as examples, and evaluate their applicability.

In practice, BIM models become less important once the construction phase is complete, although the information that they contain could continue to be very useful for operation and ownership. Infrastructure operators, in particular, use geographic information systems to store operational information in asset information models.

The joint use of geospatial data and building models is obviously of great benefit in many project phases, especially in approval procedures and as-built data management. These benefits are discussed, analysed, and categorised in this chapter.

6.2 Interoperability

Interoperability is a prerequisite for the joint use of BIM and GIS. Because the term "interoperability" is central to the problem, a phenomenology that is neutral towards BIM and GIS is used: The requirements defined in ISO 11354-1 (Advanced automation technologies and their application – Requirements for achieving process interoperability in manufacturing organisations – Part 1: Framework for enterprise interoperability (ISO, 2011)) formulated categories of interoperability, which form the common thread of this chapter. Even though this framework was actually developed as an analysis template for interoperability between companies, it is also suitable for analysing application domains, such as BIM and GIS.

As shown in Figure 6.1, the concept of interoperability encompasses more than just the ability to exchange data between computer systems. Investigations into BIM/GIS interoperability have been carried out from the perspectives of "data", "services", "processes", and "business operations". The second axis of the evaluation categories is divided into the values "conceptual", "technological", and "organisational". The difference between "conceptual" and "technological" helps, for example, to differentiate between mathematical concepts of coordinate transformation and their technical implementation in data exchange formats and software when it comes to georeferencing BIM models. The third axis, "approach", distinguishes between the three following interoperability approaches:

- Integrated interoperability, which is when concepts in both domains can be used in a common form, data can be converted, and processes and business models can be adapted. A typical example is the conversion of

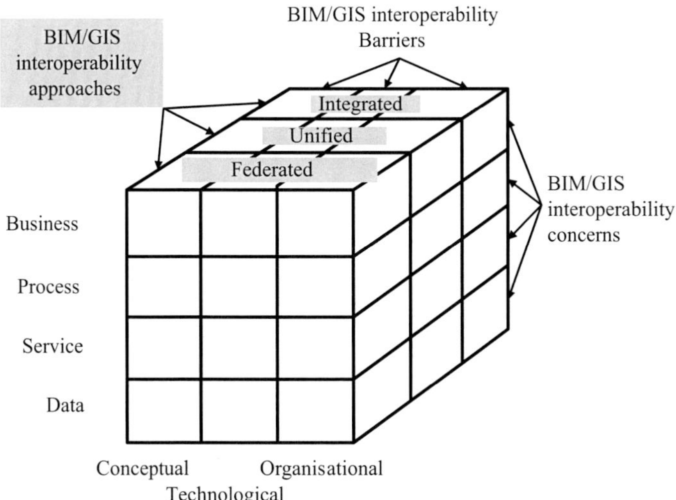

FIGURE 6.1
The categories of interoperability are described in ISO 11354-1 as a multidimensional challenge and serve as classification criteria for the many interoperability aspects of BIM/GIS.

geographic information into IFC (GIS→BIM) or the transfer of building floor plans into GIS (BIM→GIS);

- Unified interoperability, which is when both domains share a reference vocabulary, reference concept, or metadata. Typical examples are intermediate formats for common data environments (CDEs) or ontology mapping in the semantic web. Standardised approaches are currently the subject of research and could improve BIM and geospatial interoperability in the future;
- Federated interoperability, which is when there are no common metamodels and parts of the different resources are only merged during use/the execution of specific tasks. The dynamic adaptation of the forms is done by the applications at runtime and relationships between systems may need to be added ad hoc or manually. For example, 3D building models and geospatial data could be interpreted and linked by software without any conversions. This technically challenging task requires complex software and, ideally, clear rules for linking source documents.

However, the general-purpose ISO 11354-1 framework is not always precisely applicable to BIM and GIS interoperability. When in doubt, a practical explanation is preferred to the strict use of the framework. Strict use is further complicated by the fact that the terms "integrated", "unified", and "federated" are used very differently in the scientific literature. In Beck et al. (2021), the different, and sometimes contradictory, use of terms related to interoperability concepts is described in detail.

The ISO 11354-1 standard only provides an abstract framework. This chapter, therefore, also addresses the specific categories of BIM and GIS integration that were developed in the joint working groups ISO/TC 211 (Geographic information/Geomatics) and ISO/TC 59/SC 13 (Organisation and Digitisation of Information about Buildings and Civil Engineering Works, Including (BIM) and published in the Technical Report ISO/TR 23262:2021 (ISO, 2021). A summary of this technical report can be found in Clemen (2022).

6.3 Aspects of BIM and GIS Interoperability

The following list names, supplements, and explains the technical aspects listed in ISO/TR 23262:2021 for interoperability between BIM and GIS. This list can be used as a guideline for meetings, for example, if building models (BIM) and geodata (GIS) are to be used together in IT projects.

- Metamodels for Object Creation.

  Abstract formal concepts, such as the structures of objects/features, object-oriented inheritance, the structure of attributes, and the definitions of enumerations, may differ fundamentally. Typical examples for GIS are the General Feature Model (ISO 19109, 2015) and IFC kernels (ISO 16739, 2024a), or metamodels for data catalogues (ISO 12006-3, 2022).

- Metamodels for Semantics.

  GIS structures the level of meaning in a strictly object-structured or object-oriented manner according to the General Feature Model (ISO 19109, 2015), i.e., with classes and attributes. BIM also uses standardised feature groups and cross-class feature servers. Prominent examples are the buildingSMART Data Dictionary (bSDD) and national "PropertyServer", which are provided by national standardisation bodies, for example.

- Granularity of Information (LoX Concepts).

  The two domains have very different methods for describing the granularity of information. In BIM, the concept of "Level of Information Need" (ISO 7817-1, 2024b) is used to define the depth of information required for each planning stage in projects. The geometric expressiveness (Level of Geometry; LoG) and semantic depth (Level of Information; LoI), as well as the type and manner of related documents (Level of Documentation; LOD), are defined for each type in models. This perspective is not adopted for geospatial data if it is provided via spatial data infrastructure (SDI). Here, granularity is understood as a property (not a need) of resources and is often referred to as the Level of Detail (LOD).

- Georeferencing: Mathematical and Conceptual Models.

  Building models are georeferenced if the transformation parameters between the building coordinate systems and geodetic coordinate reference systems are known. There are different mathematical and conceptual concepts for describing these transformation parameters. The mathematical concepts and data exchange formats, the algorithms of CAD (Computer Aided Design)/GIS/BIM software, and the graphical user interfaces are implemented very differently (see Chapter 5).

- Geometric 3D Representations.

  Lines, surfaces, and volumes can be mapped in 3D embedding spaces using different mathematical concepts, calculation rules, and data formats. BIM and GIS usually use different geometric representation types. When used together, evaluation systems must be able to interpret a variety of representation types. In most cases, building models (BIM) are used various CAD modelling methods, such as parametric modelling, constructive solid geometry (CSG), and boundary representation (B-Rep) (see Chapter 2). On the other hand, 3D geospatial data are usually provided exclusively via B-Rep.

- Geometric Representations with Dimensional Changes (2D, 2.5D, and 3D).

  Geospatial data (for example, cadastres), environmental data, and measured site plans are predominantly 2D. For visualisation and spatial coordination in BIM software, geometric representation forms may need to be adapted into 3D. For example, 2D geodata can be draped onto digital terrain models (DTMs) or 2D polygons can be extruded into flat solids.

- Topological Relations between Objects.

  This aspect refers, in particular, to topological relationships (e.g., "lies in", "touches", "connects", etc.) that are explicitly stored in datasets. These explicit topological relations between components are often lost during data conversion due to interoperability problems or they are incorrectly decoded by reading systems.

- Alignment/Linear Referencing.

  Topographical objects can additionally or alternatively be georeferenced via alignment in linear reference systems. The coordinates are then given via longitudinal and transverse values in relation to the alignment lines. Here, too, the conversion between different representation models must be checked carefully because linear referencing in railroad construction is not a purely mathematical construct. Administrative units, such as alignment designation and the direction of travel, must also be conceptualised. Gaps or jumps in mileage due to conversion measures often place high demands on automatic conversion.

- Spatial Project Structures.

  In BIM, projects are structured by parcels, buildings, floors, or rooms, for example. These topological subdivisions are not supported in GIS that are purely feature-based. Workarounds are needed to use these subdivisions in GIS because standard GIS schemas do not recognise these BIM concepts.

- Temporal Structure/Planning, Construction, and Operating Phases.

  Numerous GIS systems and standards support spatiotemporal data. There is currently no similarly established codification of time modelling in BIM. Although IFC supports temporal data types and processes, these are rarely used in practice and are poorly supported by the software.

- Metadata for Information Delivery.

  Metadata are data about data. Typical metadata generally refer to authors, creation dates, etc. In addition, subject-specific metadata can be agreed; for GIS, for example, metadata would include acquisition dates, measurement methods, or license models. In BIM, workflow metadata are in accordance with ISO 19650 (2018). Meanwhile, 19650-1 plays a special role; for example, metadata on processing status include "work in progress", "shared", "published", or "archived".
- Data Formats/Encoding.

  Different data formats within the same information model (e.g., IFC as a STEP physical file, XML (Extensible Markup Language), RDFs (resource description frameworks), or CityGML as XML or JSON (JavaScript Object Notation)) can sometimes lead to interoperability problems. These problems at the encoding level are usually easy to solve for software developers.
- Link Concepts between Structured Model Elements.

  Information containers for linked document delivery (ICDDs) are a trend in general information technology that is to "link rather than convert". Linking models can promote interoperability between BIM, GIS, and surveying. Link models connect federated models via persistent links to extend and share their information spaces, with the goal of automatically evaluating related information through combined data queries and filtering. The ISO 21597-1 standard (ISO, 2020) provides a formal framework for this.
- Web-Based Data Services.

  Geospatial data can often be queried via web services within spatial data infrastructure (SDI). Prominent examples are the Web Map Service (WMS) for rendered maps or the Web Feature Service for vector objects. Today, these services are increasingly being supplemented by OGC (Open Geospatial Consortium) API services. There are no comparable, manufacturer-neutral standards for querying building models. However, there has been a great amount of research on this topic. In the long term, IFC schema should also become web-enabled.
- System Architectures.

  The interaction of hardware, software, interfaces, and data is solved very differently in the application domains of BIM and GIS. Model-driven architectures (MDAs) and service-oriented architectures (SOAs) are established for the geospatial domain. Organisational structures, such as states or large infrastructure companies, favour uniform data provision. BIM, on the other hand, is dominated by file-based data exchanges, possibly bundled in containers, such as in ISO 19650 (ISO, 2018). With BIM, central data management takes place in CDEs.

- Collaboration with BCF.

  The BIM Collaboration Format (BCF) stores issue-related communication and models separately. BCF uses element identifiers to refer to individual building components. For example, BCF is used when design errors, quality defects, collisions, or inspection comments are involved. In BCF files or BCF database endpoints, defect descriptions, processors, statuses, screenshots, and camera positions on 3D models are also stored, in addition to the IDs of affected components. The BCF is not currently used for geospatial data or GIS.

- Organisation of Project and Business Processes.

  As shown in Figure 6.1, interoperability barriers can also exist at an administrative level in BIM projects and recurring business processes. The topics of geodata in BIM and building models for geodata are therefore not only of a technical nature but also generally require communication at the management level and, if necessary, adaptations in business models and business processes.

- Ownership, License Models, Open Data, and Database Rights.

  Data that are incorporated into BIM projects can have different, sometimes contradictory, license models. The right to use and liability claims to BIM data tend to be agreed upon under private law, for example, in special BIM contract terms. Geospatial data published by public authorities in Germany, for example, are subject to "Data License Germany", which is similar to CC BY-SA 4.0 Deed Attribution-ShareAlike 4.0 International. In BIM projects, architectural designs may be subject to creative copyright protection.

6.4 Basic Terms for BIM and GIS

While there is a standardised terminology for established GIS, BIM terms have not yet been finally codified due to the current paradigm shift from drawing-based to model-based planning, construction, and operation. The concepts and categories of interoperability between BIM and GIS are also discussed inconsistently in the literature. This applies to all types of research examined.

Many authors have pointed out that the two acronyms BIM and GIS are not comparable on the same level. The term BIM focuses on information models, while the term GIS describes a type of software. For this purpose, Donaubauer et al. (2022) provided the overview presented in Table 6.1.

Other authors have mentioned the information models of geospatial information modelling (GIM) (Herle et al., 2020) and, depending on model

TABLE 6.1

The terms "BIM" and "GIS" are not strictly phenomenologically comparable. (According to Donaubauer et al., 2022 and additions from Herle et al., 2020.)

Domain	Architecture, Engineering, and Construction (AEC) and Facility Management (FM)	Geospatial
Method	Building information modelling (BIM)	Geospatial information modelling (GIM): Urban information modelling (UIM); Topography information modelling (TIM); Network information modelling (NIM); Landscape information modelling (LIM)
Software and System	CAD (+ simulators)	GIS (+ simulators)
Data models	e.g., Industry Foundation Classes (IFC)	e.g., CityGML

content, land information modelling (LIM) for landscape planning (Abdirad and Lin, 2015) or network information modelling (NIM) for when network topology is the focus of the infrastructure (Taesombut and Chien, 2007). In the context of cartography, the term topographic information modelling (TIM) is also used, e.g., in the German ATKIS (Amtliches Kartographisches Informationssystem).

The compound acronym "GeoBIM" has been used by numerous authors for many years to describe GIS and BIM integration approaches, albeit with slightly different content (Zobl and Marschallinger, 2008, Laat and van Berlo, 2011, Noardo, Ellul et al., 2020). Recently, the software products of the companies ESRI and Autodesk, which are used to integrate building models and geospatial data, have also been marketed under the names ESRI GeoBIM^{SM} and Autodesk Construction Cloud.

In the following sections, the academically more correct terms of GIM, TIM, etc. are avoided in favour of the terms "BIM" and "GIS", which are commonly used in professional practice.

Overview studies by Liu et al. (2017), Wang et al. (2019), and Garramone et al. (2020) used quantitative analyses of literature databases and search terms to investigate the extend of research on the integration of BIM and GIS. The authors of these overview studies used the bibliographic databases Web of Science[2] and Scopus[3].

Liu et al. (2017) showed the fundamental differences between BIM and GIS in their comprehensive literature review. The distinction has been made in scientific research by model intention, user type, use case, software system, semantic and geometric representation, granularity/detail, application focus, stage of development, spatial scale, and method for storing and accessing coordinate information. This non-exhaustive list covers a large part of the interoperability problem. According to Liu et al. (2017), integration can be classified by approaches at the data level, process level, and application level. In future, particular attention should be paid to solution approaches that use semantic web technology to integrate specialist models at the application level. Scientific publications have described integration concepts as necessary and useful in many application areas, such as 3D cadastres, location-based services (LBSs), asset management, monument preservation, building land procurement, environmental analyses, and occupational health and safety.

Wang et al. (2019) quantitatively analysed numerous scientific publications in terms of sustainability. The literature on data integration, energy management, urban management, and life cycle management was examined. Their emphasis on the need for common semantics (e.g., class names, characteristics, etc.) for integration platforms is interesting. This approach is also taken, for example, by the feature database of the BIM Portal Deutschland[4].

Garramone et al. (2020) identified three further modes of BIM and GIS integration:

1. BIM guides while GIS supports;
2. GIS guides while supports BIM;
3. BIM and GIS are equally involved.

These three modes are, to a certain extent, guided by the problem definition. Garramone et al. (2020) analysed the scientific literature, focusing on the aspect of infrastructure asset management. Based on 54 evaluated specialist articles, the authors found that many publications each used BIM and GIS as tools for asset management. However, the joint use of BIM and GIS for asset management was identified by the authors as a challenge. As shown in Figure 6.2, only 16.6% of the 54 thematically relevant publications addressed the benefits of the integration of BIM and GIS for asset management.

In the EuroSDR GeoBIM project[5], BIM and GIS integration was the focus of a research network for the International Society for Photogrammetry and Remote Sensing (ISPRS) and the European Association for Spatial Data Research (EuroSDR). Different scenarios in European partner countries (excluding Germany) were analysed and the exchange of information with the manufacturer-neutral information models of CityGML (city models) and IFC (building models) was tested (Ellul et al., 2018). Noardo, Harrie et al. (2020) showed in detail how software systems interpret the georeferencing of building models in the IFC format. For this purpose, they used the LoGeoRef classification of Clemen and Görne (2019). They also showed how and with which software tools building models can be georeferenced. As already described by Biljecki and Tauscher (2019), the actual quality of the input data

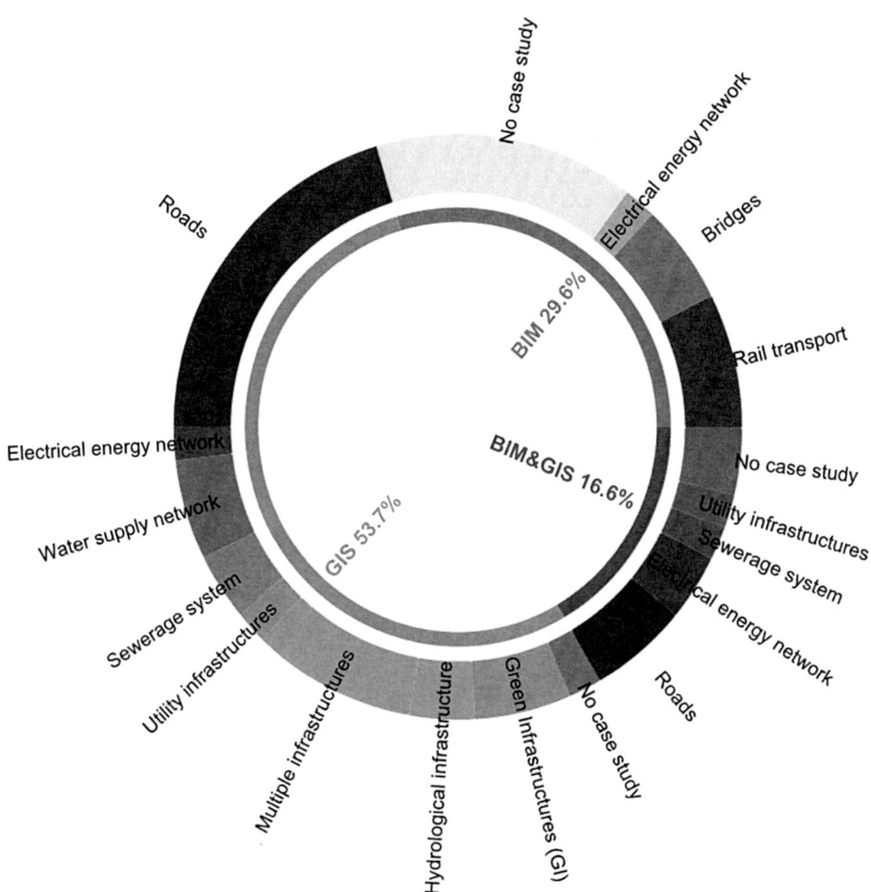

FIGURE 6.2
Garramone et al. identified a research gap in 2020 because only 16.6 % of the 54 publications (1991–2020) on the topic of infrastructure asset management that were analysed addressed the synergetic benefits of joint BIM and GIS use.

(document instances) is crucial for practical implementation, in addition to the potential convertibility of information models (schemas). The approach described in Noardo, Harrie et al. (2020) is structured according to the following key questions:

1. How does BIM software (and other programs) support vendor-neutral IFC?
2. What options are there for georeferencing BIM data?
3. What support is there for CityGML within GIS and other tools?

4. What conversion options (software and methods, both IFC to CityGML and CityGML to IFC) are available?

The authors noted that tools for georeferencing are generally not used transparently and that the users of the software have few control or configuration options. Furthermore, it was shown that the georeferencing of BIM models is currently not clearly standardised when it comes to geometric accuracy, as well as the unambiguous use of certain classes and attributes in IFC. For the conversion of building models (IFC) into city models (CityGML), only the three systems IFC2CityGML, ESRI ArcGIS Pro, and FME Desktop were examined. None of these three programs could correctly convert IFC components completely and semantically. The authors pointed out that conversion must currently be verified by experts and checked for success in each individual case. In addition to the scientific questions, the test data created for the GeoBIM benchmark are also very useful (Noardo, Harrie et al., 2020).

6.5 Integration of Information Models

A key issue in the integration of BIM and GIS is the underlying information models and their direct transfer. Beck et al. (2021) developed a clear diagram of the types of integration (Figure 6.3).

The first type is "Conversion", which is usually found in the literature between the IFC and CityGML data formats (Gnädinger and Roth, 2021; Wilhelm, 2020; Zhu et al., 2021). The second type of integration is "Extension", which involves extending one information model with certain

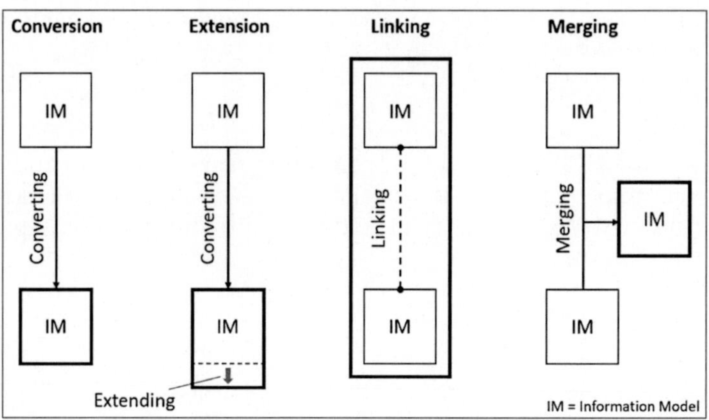

FIGURE 6.3
Diagram of four types of data integration according to Beck et al. (2021).

parts of another. This approach is application-specific and not necessarily transferable to other processes. In contrast, the commonly considered solution of linking can be found in many publications (Beck et al., 2021; Liu et al., 2017). The last, and probably most complex, method is "Merging", which involves creating new information models that contain both incoming information models.

Esser and Borrmann (2021) stated that container-based information management, according to ISO 19650-1, is inadequate if model updates are made at the component level but are not propagated to other containers due to insufficient linking. The authors named the following as the material basis of formal links for infrastructure management: The spatial structure of projects (breakdown structure), linear reference systems, and railway-specific classification systems. The article thus highlights future developments for the technical underpinning of BIM Level 3, i.e., integrated information management.

In numerous overview studies on the integration of BIM and GIS, e.g., Djuedja et al. (2019) and Herle et al. (2020), standardisation has been identified as the key to successful BIM and GIS integration.

6.6 Relevant Standards for BIM and GIS Interoperability

As described in Clemen (2022), numerous efforts to integrate BIM and GIS are currently taking place in standardisation and pre-standardisation committees. These efforts are embedded within paradigmatic changes in GIS standardisation, e.g., the established OGC web standards, such as the Web Feature Service (WFS), being supplemented and partially replaced by the new OGC API. These new GIS standards can be better used in distributed IT infrastructure and across domains. Therefore, they are important candidates for future GIS and BIM integration. The combined activities of the OGC 3D Information Management Working Group[6] of the OGC are also relevant for the BIM sector. OGC activities are explicitly aimed at the integration of "Architecture, Engineering, Construction, Operation and Ownership" (AECOO). Pre-standardisation at OGC and buildingSMART deals with BIM and GIS integration through the Integrated Digital Built Environment (IDBE) Working Group.

Various aspects of international standardisation for building information models (BIM) and geospatial data (GIS) are compared in the following section. However, a 1:1 comparison is not possible because the two standard biotopes are structured very differently. The GIS standards from OGC and ISO TC211 (Geographic information/Geomatics) constitute a well-coordinated and more technical framework that is strongly oriented towards the model driven architecture (MDA) paradigm. The aim of the more than 60 modularised

GIS standards is primarily uniform, efficient, and quality-assured software development. ISO 19101 (ISO, 2014a) describes the comprehensive standard work of ISO TC211 and explains general concepts, such as interoperability, requirements, abstraction, and profiles.

The BIM standards are rather loosely organised and not optimally coordinated. Some BIM standards, such as IFC, BCF, and bSDD, are also aimed at software development. IFC contains many concepts in a single standard that are distributed across several GIS-related standards. Many BIM standards address project management. ISO 19650-1 (ISO, 2018) specifies a general BIM project structure. Other management standards on BIM terms, model detailing, processes, and data transfer, as well as shared data environments, are grouped around ISO 19650 and support it but can also be considered separately.

6.6.1 Conceptual Schemas

In the OGC and ISO/TC 211 standards, Unified Modelling Language (UML; ISO/IEC 19505-2, 2012a) is used for conceptual modelling. The EXPRESS modelling language (ISO 10303-11, 2019a) currently dominates BIM standards; however, at buildingSMART, there are currently efforts to also encourage the use of UML in the future (van Berlo et al., 2021).

6.6.2 Metamodels for Object Formation

The meta-concepts for describing real-world objects with UML are specified for GIS in ISO 19109. The General Feature Model defines the abstract concepts for features, coverage, characteristics, attributes, and relations, as well as their implementation in UML. There are currently no comparably differentiated and independent metamodels for BIM. ISO 12006-3 (Building construction – Organisation of information about construction works – Framework for object-oriented information) for classification systems and feature databases and the IFC kernel schema for the exchange of building models perform similar functions. Jetlund et al. (2020) showed how the abstract concepts of BIM and GIS can be harmonised and linked at the conceptual schema level.

6.6.3 Semantics

The specification of the semantics, i.e., meaning, of spatial features must be differentiated from their geometric, topological, and graphic information, as well as from metadata. Semantics are primarily expressed through classification and attribution. In GIS standards, semantics are specified according to the rules of ISO 19107 (Spatial Schema (ISO, 2019b)) and ISO 19109 (Rules for application schema (ISO, 2015)) in the special application schemas. For example:

- OGC CityGML specifies classes, attributes, and relations for the semantic modelling of buildings, bridges, tunnels, street furniture, urban objects, land use, terrain, transport, vegetation, and waterways. Donaubauer et al. (2022) comprehensively presented the new CityGML 3.0 concepts in the context of BIM and GIS integration;
- The EU initiative INSPIRE[7] conceptualises administrative units, transport networks, geology, mineral resources, the distribution of species and protected areas, etc. in order to create common environmental policy by means of SDI;
- Other international standards, such as the Land Administration Data Model (LADM; ISO 19152) for rights and obligations to land and real estate, and the OGC LandInfra/InfraGML[8] standards for infrastructure are not currently used in Germany and have not yet been implemented in commercial software systems;
- The legally most important standards are still the national geo-standards for cadastres, mapping, defence, and infrastructure. These standards differ greatly from country to country.

Comparable layer models between metamodels and concrete application schemas do not yet exist in BIM in the form of coordinated standards but do exist in the form of schema layers within the IFC Shared Schema (ISO 16739). The schema layers are as follows:

- A domain layer for schemes of individual trades;
- An interoperability (shared) layer for general construction concepts (especially components);
- A core layer for abstract basic concepts, such as objects, features, and relationships, as well as basic concepts for building-related product data (e.g., spatial structures, grids, and levels);
- A resource layer for geometry, time, dimensions, etc., which can be used by the objects of the higher layers for modelling without being independent objects.

The classes from the IFC shared and domain layers specify entity types, such as buildings, floors, walls, doors, windows, and roofs. Schemas represent buildings or construction objects, which are referred to as entities in IFC, up to a certain level of detail. Each entity can be given property sets (IfcPropertySet) with a list of properties (IfcProperty). However, there are two major challenges with semantics in IFC:

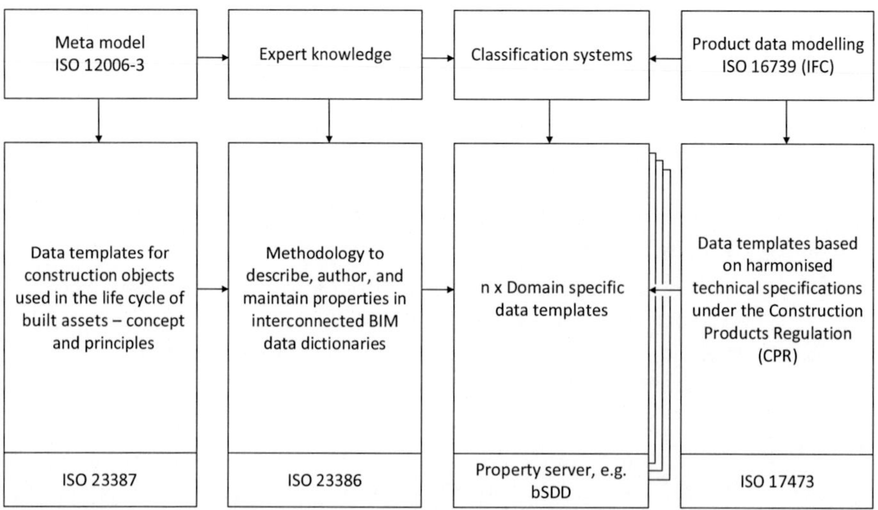

FIGURE 6.4
Overview of current BIM standards for the specification of semantics. The frameworks of ISO 12006-3, ISO 23387, and ISO 23386 can be used by experts to publish domain-specific data templates for the semantics of building components and other building-related assets in a structurally uniform manner.

- The number of IFC entities (classes), entity types (enumerations), and properties only cover a small part of the information requirements for building objects. IFC semantics are designed in a very general way and do not semantically map the requirements of national building standards;
- IFC properties are firmly linked to building models. They cannot, for example, be used separately from building models as semantic structures for component catalogues.

However, IfcPropertySet provides a mechanism for adding user-defined properties to objects (IfcObject). These user-defined properties are then syntactically compliant with IFC but not compliant with semantic information models. Standards are currently being developed in ISO/TC 59/SC 13 and CEN TC442/WG4 on how the semantics of building models can be dynamically standardised. The interaction between these standards is shown schematically in Figure 6.4.

The modularisation of the standards for semantics in openBIM projects is aimed at IFC but is not limited to it, as standardised classification systems can also be used by proprietary data formats. In the context of infrastructure data management with BIM and GIS, feature servers (or

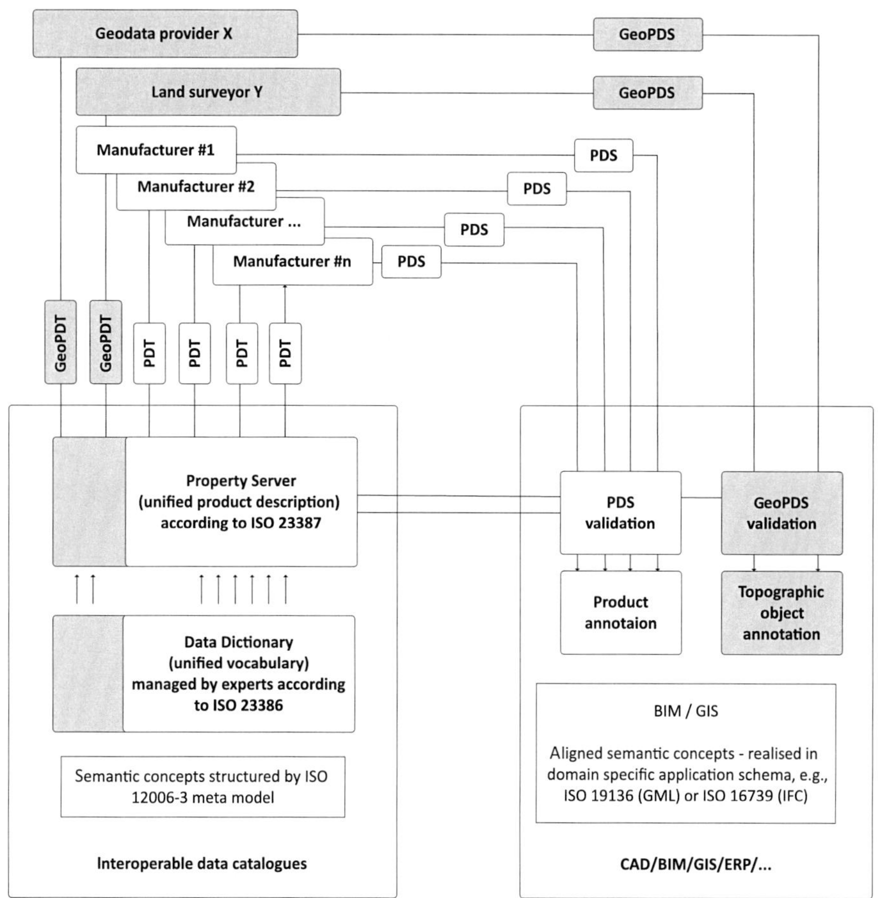

FIGURE 6.5
The BIM standards for distributed semantics with product data templates (PDTs) and product data sheets (PDSs) could, in principle, also be applied to topographic information models and used by GIS. (According to ISO/TR 23262.)

schema-external classification systems, taxonomies, and ontologies) create a good basis for coordinated, i.e., standardised, semantics. Various enterprise resource planning (ERP), CAD/BIM, and GIS software systems could share data templates (product data templates; PDTs) and product data sheets (PDSs).

Figure 6.5 outlines a possible system architecture for the shared use of semantic definitions. The server instances for dictionaries (data dictionaries) and data templates (property servers) can be administered via very different and possibly competing organisational units, such as national standardisation bodies, buildingSMART, or other associations. In Germany, the property server and property templates in the BIM portal of the Federal Ministry for

Traffic (BMDV) and the Federal Ministry of Housing, Urban Development, and Building (BMWSB) are currently very dynamic because additional properties, property groups, and property templates are continuously being imported via the federal maintenance centre.

6.6.4 Model Detailing

In GIS, the term "Level of Detail" (LOD) is used in connection with model detailing and is mostly applied to 3D city models. The LOD metric is defined in the OGC standard CityGML 3.0[9] and can be applied to building cubature and interior spaces as follows:

- LOD 0: No solids (highly generalised models);
- LOD 1: Block model (extrusion objects);
- LOD 2: Buildings with standard roof shapes and, where applicable, room volumes (realistic but still generalised models);
- LOD 3: Highly detailed exterior and/or interior models.

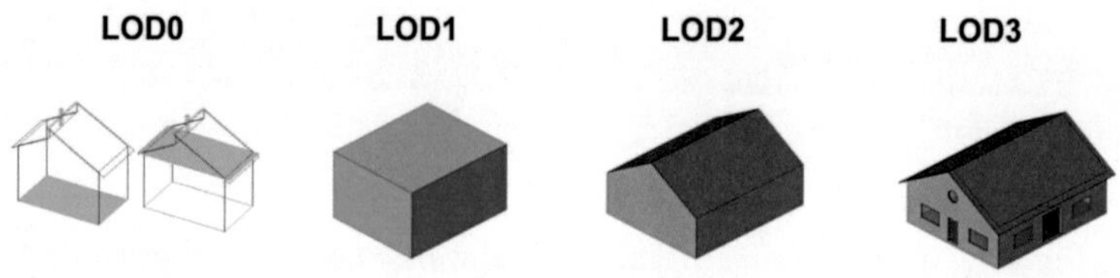

FIGURE 6.6
Representation of the same real-world building in LOD0–LOD3. (OGC Conceptual Model Users Guide[20].)

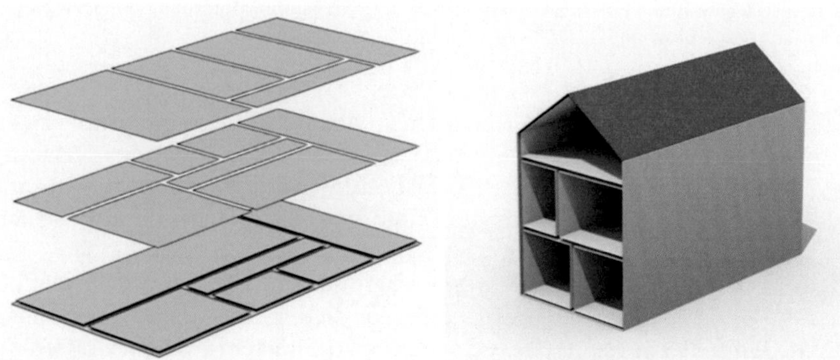

FIGURE 6.7
In CityGML standard 3.0, floor plans can be modelled in LOD0 and room volumes can be modelled in LOD2. (According to OGC and Löwner et al., 2016.)

CityGML model instances can contain the same buildings in multiple LOD representations. The LOD definition is used in CityGML 3.0 for the integration of detailed building models (Figure 6.7) into city models (Löwner et al., 2016).

The description of model detailing for BIM was initially largely shaped in the US. As early as 2008, US associations agreed the Level of Development Specification for Building Information Models in the BIM Forum[10]. To prevent the misunderstanding of "over-regulation", the standard states that the Level of Development (LoD) specification is not a compilation of requirements as to what should be modelled, or when or by whom. This is regulated in the BIM execution plan (BEP). Rather, the BIM Forum provides a common language with which users can define requirements for their own companies or projects. The standard is aligned with the requirements of architecture and describes successive model development stages, from an initial room concept (LoD100) to detailed implementation planning with all of the relevant technical details (LoD400).

The European CEN/TC 442/WG 2/TG1 committee developed BIM definition levels for the detailing of information exchange, the so-called Level of Information Need (LOIN), which are now published as ISO 7817-1. The term "Level of Information Need" changes the perspective: While the BIM Forum LoD refers to the degree of completion as a property of the models themselves, the LOIN explicitly includes the expectations (need) of information providers in the title of the standard. The standard does not define a metric but differentiates categories to describe the depth of information requirements. As shown schematically in Figure 6.9, the geometric level of detail (LoG) considers dimensions, positional references, and, if applicable, visual representations and parametric behaviour. In addition, the type of object identification (i.e., name, ID, etc.) and the type and structure of object classification and attribution must be defined by the Level of Information (LoI). Finally, the Level of Documentation (DOC) regulates the level of detail and scope of (external) documents that are supplied in addition to virtual building models. Examples include room books, inventory lists, written reports, data sheets, manuals, photos, and detailed drawings.

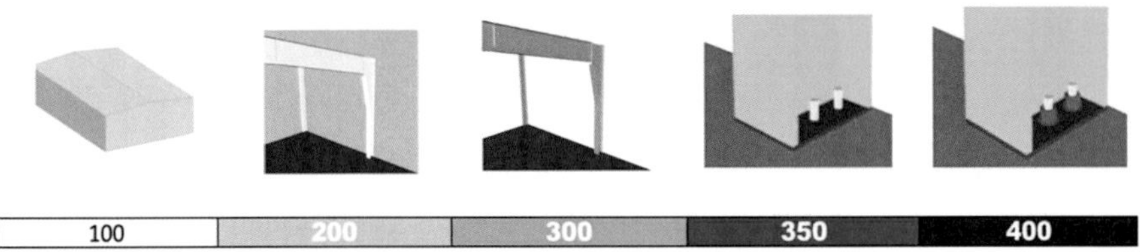

FIGURE 6.8
Simplified representation of model development in the "Level of Development" (LoD) of the BIM Forum of US construction industry associations. (bimforum.org.)

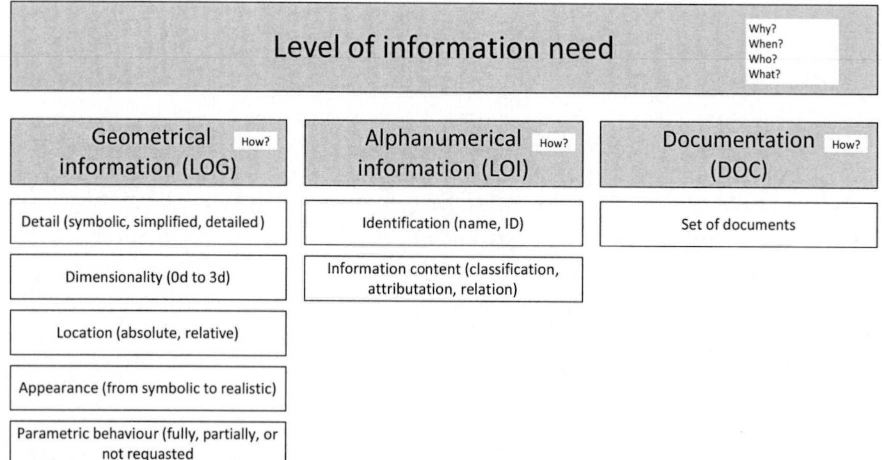

FIGURE 6.9
Concepts and principles of the Levels of Information Need (LOIN) have been standardised in 7817-1.

In purely practical terms, the ISO 7817-1 standard can already be used as a checklist to ensure that all essential aspects of the depth of information requirements have been discussed. It can also serve as a framework for application-specific standards for information requirements in the future. The CEN/TC 442/WG 2 is currently working on expanding the standards on the depth of information requirements. Part 2 will be written as an explanatory application manual with examples. For Part 3, a computer-interpretable XML schema is being developed that standardises the digital exchange of the depth of information requirements between software systems.

The LOIN system can be used for infrastructure data management with BIM and GIS on the basis of buildingSMART's BIM Classes of Traffic Alignments 2.0 (Brommer et al., 2022). Recommended further developments of the standard, with regard to LOG, are as follows:

- The LOG category "Dimensionality" describes the topological dimensions of information objects (wireframes, surface models, volume models, etc.). This should be supplemented by the category "Dimension of the Embedding Space" with the selection list (2D, 3D). For example, lines (topological dimension 1) can be modelled in both 2D and 3D embedding spaces. This essential statement on information requirement depth cannot currently be expressed but is of the utmost importance for GIS because most geospatial data are only two-dimensional;
- The LOG category "Dimensionality" should indicate geometric objects of dimension 2.5 DTM. It is often wrongly assumed that DTMs (e.g., TINs,

grids, longitudinal or transverse profiles, etc.) are three-dimensional. However, ISO 19123 (ISO, 2023a) uses the term "coverage", which for DTMs means that each point in the horizontal plane is functionally assigned exactly one height coordinate (z or H). Therefore, DTMs have no real 3D dimensionality;

- It is currently not clear whether ordered objects should/can be modelled and instantiated by means of prototyping (e.g., from component libraries) or as individual objects. This is of great importance for the selection of GIS software tools and the organisation of surveying work.

Based on the concept of LoGeoRef from *ISO/TR 23262* (ISO, 2021), the following are two further requirements for the specification of information requirement depth with LOIN:

- Identifiers for absolute coordinate reference systems must be specified, ideally with concepts simplified for BIM from ISO 19111;
- The type of transformation rule in project base points must be defined, which may also have a horizontal rotation (true north) and a translation for the Earth-related height of the project base points;
- The type of height system (i.e., Cartesian z-coordinate or Earth-related height (e.g., normal height)) must be specified.

The concepts of the Level of Accuracy (LOA) standard (USIBD, 2019), for example, the separation of measurement accuracy and maximum model deviation between measurement and modelling (see Figure 6.10), should also be included in the LOIN standard as a category for measurement accuracy should be introduced within the LOG for BIM/GIS as-built documentation based on the US Institute of Building Documentation (USIBD) LOA.

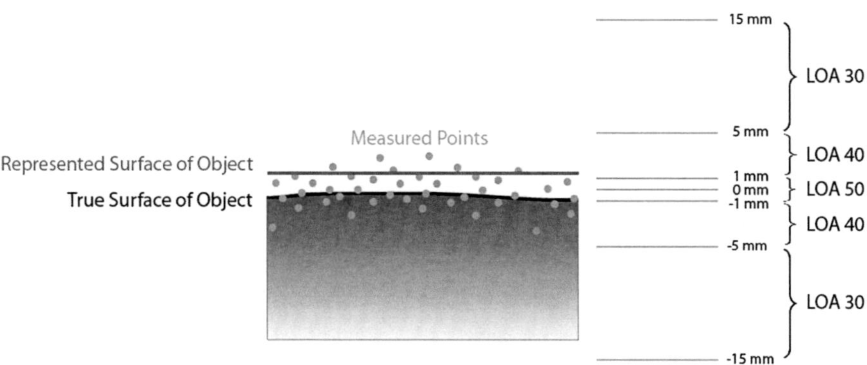

FIGURE 6.10
The LOA standard of the USIBD, showing the measurement accuracy and maximum model deviation separately.

6.6.5 Geometric and Topological Representation

The complexity of the mutual transfer of geometric representation types between BIM, GIS, and collaboration platforms is often underestimated. This transformation is not a simple 1:1 schema mapping. The variety of geometric representation types used (e.g., mathematical models and computer representations) in BIM and GIS results from different model intensions. The suitable geometric representation of individual objects (i.e., entities, features, real-world objects, components, etc.) is strongly correlated with semantics. A wall in BIM has a different meaning from a wall in GIS; therefore, it also requires different geometry and topology concepts. The options for representing geometry and topology are also used very differently in the standards.

The OGC/ISO Spatial Schema (ISO, 2019b) is the most important conceptual model for describing, displaying, and manipulating geographic vector data for GIS. The standard includes the following:

- Coordinate reference systems for describing positions in global and local contexts;
- Basic geometric elements (e.g., GM_Point, GM_Curve, GM_Surface GM_Solid, etc.);
- The geometric representation of objects as basic elements, as complex or composite (e.g., GM_CompositePoint, GM_CompositeCurve, GM_CompositeSurface, GM_CompositeSolid, etc.), and as aggregates (e.g., GM_MultiPoint, GM_MultiCurve, GM_MultiSurface, GM_MultiSolid, etc.);
- Topological primitives (e.g., TP_Node, TP_Edge, TP_Face, TP_Ring, TP_Shell, TP_Solid, TP_EdgeBoundary, TP_FaceBoundary, TP_SolidBoundary, etc.).

In contrast to BIM standards, this GIS standard only uses boundary surface models (i.e., boundary representation (B-Rep)) to represent geometries.

Because the full implementation of the ISO 19107 (2019b) concepts is very complex, OGC and ISO developed the ISO 19125-1 standard (Simple Feature Access; ISO, 2004). With this standard, simplified, mostly two-dimensional, geometries can be stored and queried in geospatial data databases.

These central conceptual standards from OGC and ISO are the conceptual basis for important application schemas, such as the OGC standard CityGML[11]; however, this restricts some representations. For example, GM_Curve must be linear, GM_Surface must be planar, and topological concepts (i.e., TP_XXX) are not used.

The conceptual basis for the openBIM IFC standard is the Standard for the Exchange of Product Model Data (STEP). In this comprehensive collection of standards, Part 42 (ISO, 2019a) describes concepts for geometric and topological data structures. The standards are designed for the exchange of complex CAD models with high demands on numerical stability and modelling flexibility. This means that model intentions differ those of from GIS concepts, which are primarily intended for the small-scale provision of environmental data. Each product in the STEP context can have different and multiple geometric and topological representations (multiple representations).

The representation of geometries in ISO 16739-1 (IFC) is essentially based on STEP (Part 42) but is adapted for the construction industry. IFC schemas are formulated in the meta-language EXPRESS. The naming convention for entities (classes) in IFC utilises inner majuscules and IFC prefixes. The original STEP entities that use multiple inheritance or non-exclusive inheritance (i.e., the AND or ANDOR subtype constraints) have been adapted for IFC. Certain geometry representations (e.g., pcurves) have been replaced by simple representations. The "name" attribute does not have to be specified for geometric and topological representation elements in IFC.

The IFC standard is divided into the three modules of core data, shared element data, and domain-specific data schemas for the representation of (real) objects in building systems. All geometric and topological resources must be referenced by objects that have global IDs.

The type of geometries used in IFC are characterised by the following:

- The use of multiple Cartesian coordinate systems, with each display context defining cascading coordinate transformations, e.g., across projects, buildings, floors, and components;
- Many possible basic geometric items (geometric_representation_item) for dimensions 1, 2, and 3;
- Various options for describing geometric relationships (e.g., BRep, CSG, extrusion, sweep, etc.);
- Many topological elements.

From a practical GIS perspective, the term "topology" encompasses neighbourhood relationships in the following two forms:

- Explicitly stored relations, e.g., for road or pipeline networks. For example, node-edge models or higher-value graphs are stored in geospatial databases and analysed in GIS. In GIS standards, topological data structures are standardised under TP_Primitive and TP_Complex;
- Implicit topological relationships between two geometric features that are calculated on-demand by geospatial databases or GIS. A typical example is the query of whether two polygons (e.g., noise zones and houses) touch or penetrate each other. The main standard for topological queries is the Simple Feature Access standard (ISO, 2004).

The term "topology" is understood somewhat differently in BIM, as follows:

- Data structures for describing components, especially for boundary surface models (B-Rep) in the IFCTOPOLOGYRESOURCE package of IFC (ISO, 2024a);
- Explicitly stored relations between two components that are in a decomposition relationship (e.g., IfcRelDecomposes);
- Explicitly stored relations between reference elements and components. For example, IFC uses the data type IfcGridPlacement to place components in relation to a grid;
- Project subdivision in order to understand spatially disjoint areas as units. This structure is typical seen in building construction as Project (IfcProject) → Site (IfcSite) → Building (IfcBuilding) → Storey (IfcBuildingStorey) → Space (IfcSpace). For infrastructure, the IFC schema is extended from version IFC4.3 by the concepts IfcFacility (e.g., IfcBridge, IfcRailway, etc.) and IfcFacilityPart (e.g., IfcBridgePart, IfcRailwayPart, etc.).

The great expressive power of IFC, which arises from the large number of geometric and topological forms of representation, poses a considerable problem when exchanging data between BIM and GIS. While writing software can freely select geometry types and topology concepts that are suitable to specific use cases, any IFC-reading software must, in principle, support all possible variants. This is a very high technical requirement for software development. This fact must be taken into account in technical tender criteria, for example, when it comes to transferring building models to SDIs or displaying geospatial data in CDEs.

6.6.6 Metadata

Metadata support established methods in GIS for managing, publishing, and filtering geoinformation. Metadata are used to define the properties, structures, and relationships of datasets. The GIS metadata standard ISO 19115 (ISO, 2014b) provides a model with which information and resources with spatial references can be described in a standardised way using metadata. It defines metadata that can be used to add general information, such as quality, up-to-dateness, source, creator, and spatial extent, to the description of geospatial data. A distinction is made between mandatory and optional metadata. Metadata can help to interpret geospatial data and search for specific information within them. The standard divides metadata into packages and describes the contained classes using UML models. The appendix to the standard includes a helpful dictionary that describes the characteristics of the defined metadata.

In the field of BIM, the ISO 19650 standard (ISO, 2018) defines terms and principles for the use of building information models for business processes. The uniform use of terms reduces risk for all parties involved, saves costs, and creates useful information models over the entire life cycles of buildings. The standard contains recommendations for the specification of information management, including exchanging, recording, versioning, and organising information for all stakeholders. It describes what information management can look like, what perspectives there are on it, how information requirements are defined, and what types of information requirements there are. A distinction is made between asset and project information models. It also explains who should be involved in information management, how the provision of information should be planned, and how it should be implemented using common data environments (CDEs) over the entire life cycles of buildings.

In BIM, metadata are used to describe components more precisely, for example, by specifying materials, manufacturers, or product numbers.

However, there is no separate, uniform standard for metadata in BIM. Standardisation is needed so that metadata can be used uniformly when exchanging data between modelling, inspection, model coordination, administration, and archiving software. Harmonised standards for the content and structure of metadata are a standardisation gap for infrastructure data management with BIM and GIS.

6.6.7 Data Quality

The ISO 8000 series describes general concepts for data quality. These standards define requirements for data quality and provide recommendations for data quality management. Among other things, they specify criteria for data quality, such as completeness, consistency, accuracy, and timeliness. For the geometric, topological, and semantic quality of CAD models in mechanical engineering (but also in civil engineering and geoinformation), the many, highly formalised checking rules of the SASIG Product Data Quality Guidelines for the Global Automotive Industry (ISO, 2006) can be used for model checking.

The GIS standard for data quality is ISO 19157 (Geographic information – Data quality; ISO, 2023b). This standard specifies the general principles, methods, and procedures for data quality management in geographic information and contains requirements for data quality, including the aspects of the completeness, accuracy, timeliness, coherence, and availability of geospatial data. ISO 19157 also describes the requirements for the assessment of data quality and provides methods for the documentation of quality information.

The BIM management standard ISO 19650 (ISO, 2018) addresses the basic concepts of data quality in common data environments (CDEs), for example, information containers should identify the following metadata: Information formats, delivery formats, information model structures, the means of structuring and classifying information, and attribute names, such as the properties of design elements and information delivery services. Due to the lack of technical standards for quality assurance, this topic is regulated at the project level and in business processes in BIM projects.

The GIS standard ISO 19157 is recommended as the guiding standard for infrastructure data management. Special concepts for the geometric inspection of 3D models can be adopted from ISO/PAS 26183:2006 in the future.

6.6.8 Link Concepts

From a general IT perspective, there is an ongoing trend from the Internet of Documents to the Internet of Data. This trend manifests itself in the numerous standards that describe the technology stack of the so-called Semantic Web[12]. In geoinformation, these technologies were anticipated at an early stage and standardised for GIS (ISO, 2012b). However, these complex IT specifications in GIS currently reflect the state of research rather than the state of established technologies. There is also a great deal of research on the Semantic Web regarding the construction industry (Beetz et al., 2021; Pauwels et al., 2017). In order to follow the trend of linking instead of converting, German[13] (Scherer and Schapke, 2014) and Dutch[14] research projects standardised ISO 21597 (ISO, 2020). This standard specifies an ontology for the general linking of documents and model elements in BIM infrastructure that is organised using information containers. The standard explicitly mentions the linking of BIM and GIS.

The ISO 21597 standard is generally used for the exchange of data on built environments within projects and is characterised by the following:

- Data from different trades are saved in their original formats (elementary models) and are not converted;
- Separate link models are also created, which describe the links between documents and/or model elements;
- Link models and elementary models form multimodels and are stored in structured multicontainers (i.e., zip-folders with link models and schemas, *.icdd);
- Defined structures for data storage in multicontainers and schemas for link models, which, for example, define different types of linking, such as binary and directed links.

There is neither conversion to other formats nor any changes in data. Links can be saved and interpreted in the Semantic Web format RDF or according to XML schemas. The underlying multimodel concept is described in detail in Fuchs (2015).

The ICDD standards could also serve as a blueprint for the future linking of building models and geospatial data in infrastructure data management.

6.6.9 Web-Based Data Services

Web-based data services play an essential role in efficient and easily accessible infrastructure data management in the field of geospatial data. With their standardised access options, they allow queries to be made to both original datasets and products derived from them. The OGC, in particular, has established a series of standards for the GIS world. These can be further subdivided into three areas: Access services (data access standards), processing services (processing standards), and visualisation services (visualisation standards). In general, these services have been established for years and are successfully used by both public and private actors in SDI worldwide.

The first standards in the area of web-based data services were published in the early 2000s (WFS version 1.1.0[15] in 2005 and WMS version 1.3.0[16] in 2004). Since the introduction of these standards, web technologies have changed rapidly in some areas. Furthermore, some of these standards are characterised by complicated and extensive specifications. In order to make the standards more future-proof and simplify their use, the OGC has started to develop a new family of OGC API standards[17]. From a technical perspective, REST, JSON, and OpenAPI are important keywords that play a central role in these new standards. Essentially, they provide the functionalities of existing standards but are intended to extend them in certain aspects in the future. The most important representatives from this family of standards are briefly presented below.

Stand-alone sections of map products are traditionally created and provided with the help of WMS. WMS interfaces have additional parameters that can be set individually, for example, to define spatial extents, coordinate reference systems, or image formats. In future, these capabilities are to be taken over by the OGC Maps API. To output the map section, WMS can access WFS internally for data retrieval.

The retrieval of original geo-features is traditionally made possible in the environments of the OGC family of web standards via WFS. WFS is, therefore, one of the access services. In addition to the geometries of provided vector data, stored attribute data are also delivered via the web. WFS that not only allow data to be queried but also changed to databases are referred to as transaction WFS or WFS-T. Retrieved data are usually provided by WFS as GML. The new standardisation for this type of web service is currently the most advanced and will be further developed in the future under the keyword OGC API features. The functionalities are basically the same as those of WFS; however, the datasets supplied are usually delivered in GeoJSON or HTML format. GML can also be supported. In contrast to the OGC Maps API, the features standard (Part 1 Core and Part 2 CRS by Reference) is already a valid OGC standard. The extension of OGC API features to include filter options and change operations is still pending and is currently only available as a draft.

In the field of GIS, vendor-neutral OGC web services have established themselves as a standard tool in distributed GIS applications. Such standardised services do not yet exist in the field of civil engineering. An initial approach to implementing such services on the basis of data stored in CDEs and processes was explained in DIN SPEC 91391-2 under the name openCDE. This approach is currently being further developed at the international level by buildingSMART, CEN, and the ISO.

CDEs are often used for collaboration within BIM projects. These are mainly used to exchange file-based data, so-called containers. As a rule, these data are downloaded locally by users and then processed further by other software applications, such as BIM authoring or checking tools. Once the work has been completed, changes made to newly created files must be manually uploaded back to the CDE in order to provide all project participants with the current work status. This manual work step is error-prone and cumbersome. In addition, users must proactively check for new work statuses before changes can be made. The aim of the openCDE initiative is to enable this data exchange to be automated within calling client software. This should ensure constantly updated data flows.

From a technical point of view, the proposed concepts are in line with the standards of the new OGC APIs. REST interfaces are also to be described using OpenAPI. Furthermore, the OAuth 2.0 standard will be used for secure authentication. OpenCDE is designed for the exchange of information containers. Information containers are defined as the smallest storage units of files or models and also contain associated metadata.

The openCDE API is currently still in the very early stages of development. The further development of the standard is to be carried out by members of the Technical Room at buildingSMART but has not yet been put into practice to any great extent.

6.6.10 Process and Project Management

As discussed in Chapter 3, the acronym "BIM" is often translated as building information modelling. In BIM methodology, the letter "M" has another meaning in addition to modelling and model: Management (Hausknecht and Liebich, 2016).

The objectives of BIM management are the efficient management, structured provision, and exchange of digital information for construction projects. Surveying and geospatial data, component catalogues, planning variants and versions, protocols, data sheets, and many other documents can be stored in project information models (PIMs) during the planning and construction phases. These data are then processed so that they can be used in asset information models (AIMs) for operation, once projects have been completed.

Ideally, information should be organised in a uniform and forward-looking manner for all phases of the life cycles of buildings, including project development, design, planning, approval, construction, and, last but not least, management.

There is currently a great need for the uniform description of tools for BIM management because the numerous specialised engineering offices and medium-sized companies in the construction industry are feeling the pressure to innovate, which has been triggered by the possibilities of the BIM method. The standardised description of contract content and management processes for collaborative digital work would provide all BIM stakeholders with a common language for the information management of construction projects, not new strict regulations.

The ISO 19650-1 standard defines concepts and principles for managing information in business processes in the built-environment sector, organised according to the BIM approach. ISO 19650-2 defines the specific requirements for information management during the delivery phase of projects.

According to ISO 19650, process-integrated information management using the BIM method is based on the definition of information exchange requirements, the planning of information delivery, and the actual delivery of information to built assets. The information is delivered in structured information containers (i.e., models, tables, databases, etc.) or unstructured information containers (i.e., data sheets, photos, etc.), which together form information models. The term "information model" is somewhat critical because in the context of software development, the term "information model" refers to the conceptual level, not the actual document instance. ISO 19650 initially names the roles of "appointing party" and "appointed party". The standard then divides the information exchange requirements of information providers into strategic (organisational information requirements; OIRs) and project-specific (project information requirements; PIRs) requirements (see Figure 6.11).

The asset information requirements (AIRs) and exchange information requirements (EIRs) are contractually agreed between the appointing party

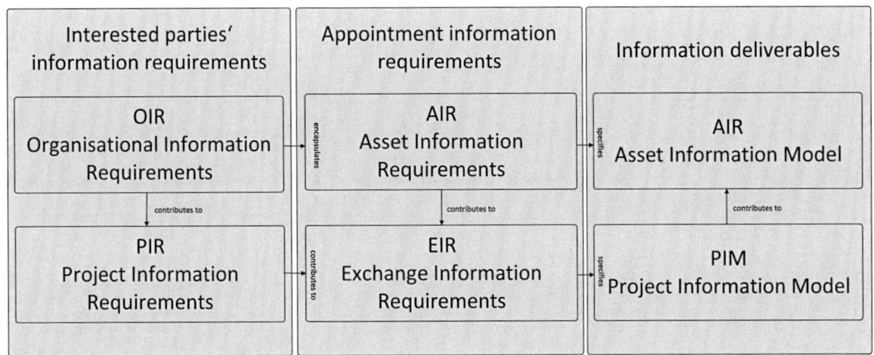

FIGURE 6.11
Hierarchy of the different information exchange requirements according to ISO 19650-1.

and appointed information providers. ISO 19650 names asset information models (AIMs) and project information models (PIMs) as deliverables in BIM processes.

The BIM method relies on clear responsibilities and the orderly transfer of data. Every stakeholder within projects expects the input data for their processes to be reliable and must ensure that their model extensions (outputs) are correctly interpreted and used by stakeholders who use the models. In the process of pre-standardisation, buildingSMART has developed a template for information delivery manuals (IDMs) that act as a framework for describing processes and data transfer points in a standardised way. The methodology and format of IDMs are defined in ISO 29481 (ISO, 2016). IDMs define "which information should be provided by whom, when and to which project participant and how" (Borrmann et al., 2021).

IDMs are, so to speak, a tool for describing subtasks that are identified in EIR, BEP, and BIM specifications. IDMs consist of a cover sheet with administrative information (author, version, etc.), a clear designation of the use case, and assignments to specific project phases. The standard describes how information delivery manuals are created. An IDM for a specific process consists of the following:

- A process map in which the who and when are clarified; and
- Exchange requirements, in which the minimum scope (what) of the data to be exchanged is defined.

The Business Process Modelling Notation (BPMN)[18] is recommended for process flow diagrams. The advantage of BPMN is that, in addition to visual and textual representations (see the left column in Figure 6.12), process

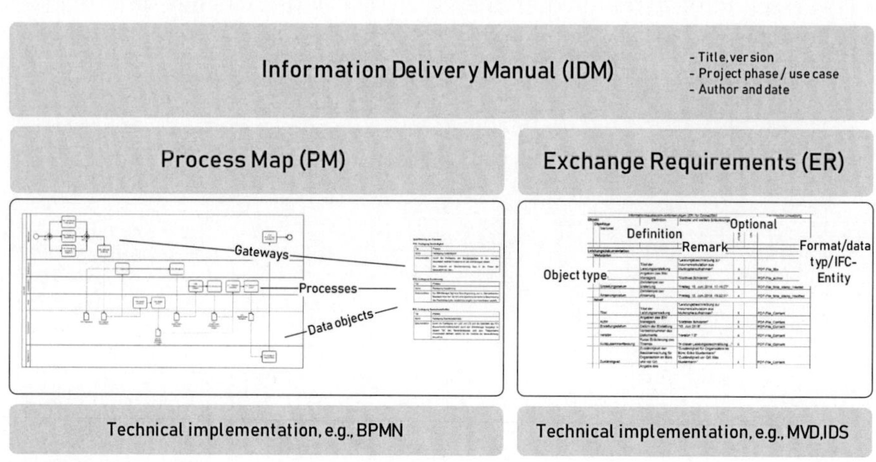

FIGURE 6.12
Schematic representation of the structure of the IDM.

definitions can be serialised and distributed as XML files. This allows defined processes to be implemented on process engines (e.g., the open-source BPMN workflow engine from Camunda). In BIM projects, the current processing statuses of process instances can then be made available to all participants (standardised) as a web service. In this way, the guiding principle of process orientation, in terms of quality assurance, is also implemented on a digital level.

For the technical implementation of information exchange requirements, the standard recommends the model view definitions (MVDs) developed by buildingSMART. MVDs define machine-readable subsets (filters) of information models and restrictions for certain relations and value ranges. MVDs can also be used for the filtering and data validation of data exchange requirements specified in IDMs. MVDs can also be used if software products are to be certified for certain data exchange scenarios. Currently buildingSMART also promotes the information delivery specifications (IDSs), which are less complex than MVDs and are mainly used to specify the semantic needs of project-related property sets (IfcPropertySet).

6.6.11 Issue Management

BCF is an open, XML-based file format for model-based communication and the coordination of conflicts between all stakeholders involved in BIM projects. The main advantage of BCF is that data exchanges for communication about models are separated from the data exchanges of the actual models. BCF is lightweight because it only transfers the three following pieces of information:

1. Screenshots as normal raster images;
2. Camera positions and their orientation within building coordinate systems;
3. Lists of objects/components from BIM model.

The format was originally developed by the two companies Solibri and Tekla (in 2009). Since 2014, it has been adopted and further developed by buildingSMART as the international openBIM standard. BCF 2.1 is currently used as the established version but BCF 3.0 has already been standardised by buildingSMART[19]. In practice, the terms "conflict", "topic", "issue", and "problem" are used synonymously.

The basis is the IFC schema and the GUIDs used in it. This makes BCF independent from BIM authoring software and separates models and communication. In addition to BIM authoring software, BCF is supported by inspection programs, such as Solibri, Tekla, Navisworks, and DESITE.

If conflicts are exchanged using the first variant, BCF files can be exported from BIM authoring software or specialist applications with BCF support after the conflicts have been created. Zip BCF files are directories and contain the following files:

- bcf.version;
- project.bcfp;
- A subfolder for each conflict, including the following:
  - markup.bcf (heart of the file)
    - Title, type, priority, deadline, description, comment, and current status;
    - Author, responsible person, and creation date;
    - References to viewpoints and snapshots;
  - viewpoint.bcfv (camera position);
  - snapshot.png (screenshot of the scene).

The bcf.version files only contain information on the BCF version used. The project.bcfp files contain the project IDs and project names so that the conflicts can be assigned to the correct projects or models. For each recorded conflict, there is a subfolder, named with the GUID of the issue. This folder contains the most important file (markup.bcf), which contains all information about the conflict. The image files of the screenshots are also stored in these folders and the corresponding camera positions are stored in the viewpoint.bcfv files. By saving the camera positions, the views of the captured screenshots can be restored for all participants in their own software.

There are two different implementation variants: XML files are exchanged or BCF servers are used via the REST API. This second variant requires a BCF server and offers the following advantages:

- Files do not have to be exchanged but are constantly synchronised with the server in the background;
- Users see clear graphical user interfaces (GUIs) in the browser or BIM software;
- Everyone involved is always up to date;
- Problems can be assigned directly to the people involved, similar to a ticket system;
- Overviews show project managers the current status of conflict processing.

There are BCF management programs that offer small plug-ins for various software and provide BCF servers.

GIS software has no standardised methods for issue management. In infrastructure data management with BIM and GIS, this gap shows an obvious need for action if geospatial data are to be used in BIM projects.

6.7 Code Compliance Checking with BIM and GIS

Approval processes, especially for large infrastructure projects, are based on checking plans against laws and political strategies. These checks are carried out on the basis of submitted documents (reports, plans, expert opinions, etc.), which could be supplemented or partially replaced by models in the future.

Fiedler (2015) used the example of the City of Vienna to estimate that around a third of the necessary checks in building approval procedures could be automated using inspection software and suitable BIM models. Special modelling guidelines and suitable reference data on the part of the building authorities could increase this proportion to around 50%.

For approval procedures for railroad infrastructure, Häußler and Borrmann (2020) examined in detail how digital construction models can be quality-assured in the categories of collisions, semantics, construction sequences, quantities, and costs so that they can be automatically checked against construction regulations. For this purpose, the authors recommended (Häußler and Borrmann, 2021) the use of a standardised process description language (i.e., BPMN) and formalised decision rules (i.e., decision model notation, DMN). The authors showed that the automated checking of geometry poses particular challenges for quality assurance, for example, if the use of coordinate systems is not clearly regulated. This is particularly important for the coordinated use of BIM and GIS in approval procedures.

Noardo et al. (2022) analysed the progress of digital building permits in an international comparison, based on the scientific literature, in a comprehensive meta-study (Figure 6.13). Starting from the paper-based process (level 1), digitalisation begins with the electronic submission of forms and 2D plans (level 2). BIM-based approval processes (Level 3) then ideally lead to the integrated use of building models and geospatial data, which is postulated as the highest level of development (Level 4) on the basis of numerous publications.

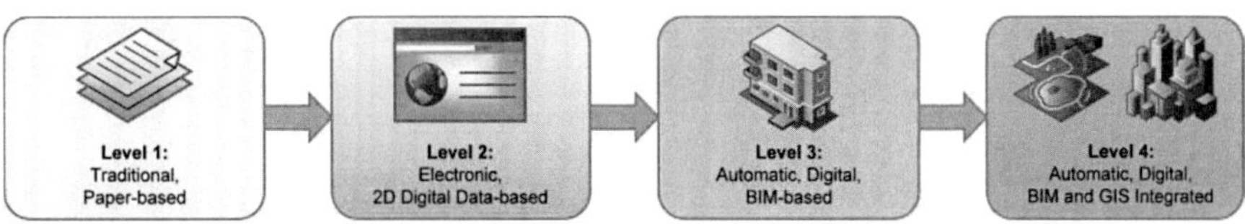

FIGURE 6.13
Four levels of applying for planning permission. (Noardo et al., 2022.)

The digitalisation of building permit procedures was seen as very promising in many of the publications because most of the process steps are currently still carried out manually and automation could save a lot of time and money. However, the procedures are very complex. The following specific requirements were extracted from over 150 scientific publications and preliminary work from the European Network for Digital Building Permit Processes (EUnet4DBP):

1. General readiness for digitalisation in public administration;
2. The existence of a concrete roadmap for fully digital approval processes;
3. Computer-interpretable legal and building regulations;
4. Availability of databases (i.e., GIS, BIM, etc.) that can be included in the processes;
5. Understanding individual process steps;
6. Internationalisation and European integration;
7. Standardisation;
8. Shared dictionaries;
9. Modelling conventions and guidelines;
10. Interoperability and APIs.

Many of the publications examined in the meta-study named the joint use of geoinformation and BIM as the most important task for implementing digital inspection and approval processes. However, a large number of publications also showed that there may be good technical and administrative solutions for this that are waiting to be implemented in practice.

Application-related solutions for calculations with GIS and BIM data have been described, for example, in Gnädinger and Roth (2021). These authors integrated a wide variety of geospatial data and building models in landscape planning and could thus examine different planning variants at a very fine granular level, e.g., with regard to various environmental regulations. Conflicts could also be identified through the intersections, whereby variants could be optimised until almost no more environmental conflicts arose.

Acknowledgements

Individual text excerpts in this article have been published by the authors in German (Clemen et al., 2023) and were based on professional collaboration with the respective co-authors and the German Centre for Rail Traffic Research (DZSF) at the Federal Railway Authority (EBA).

Notes

1 https://bmdv.bund.de/DE/Service/Publikationen/publikationen.html
2 www.webofscience.com/wos/woscc/basic-search
3 www.scopus.com/search/form.uri?display=basic#basic
4 https://via.bund.de/bim/infrastruktur/landing
5 https://3d.bk.tudelft.nl/projects/eurosdr-geobim/
6 www.ogc.org/projects/groups/3dimdwg
7 https://inspire.ec.europa.eu/
8 www.ogc.org/standards/infragml
9 www.ogc.org/standards/citygml (In CityGML 3.0, there is no longer be LOD4 because levels 0–3 also describe the detailing of the interiors of buildings).
10 https://bimforum.org/
11 www.ogc.org/standard/citygml/
12 www.w3.org/standards/semanticweb/
13 https://tu-dresden.de/bu/bauingenieurwesen/cib/forschung/researchareas/bim-technologien/index
14 www.bimloket.nl/p/483/COINS
15 www.ogc.org/standard/wfs/
16 www.ogc.org/standard/wms/
17 https://ogcapi.ogc.org/
18 www.omg.org/spec/BPMN/2.0/
19 https://github.com/buildingSMART/BCF-XML
20 https://docs.ogc.org/guides/20-066.html

Bibliography

Abdirad, H. and Lin, K.-Y. (2015) 'Advancing in Object-Based Landscape Information Modeling: Challenges and Future Needs', *Computing in Civil Engineering 2015*. Austin, Texas, June 21–23, 2015. Reston, VA, American Society of Civil Engineers, pp. 548–555.

Beck, S. F., Abualdenien, J., Hijazi, I. H., Borrmann, A. and Kolbe, T. H. (2021) 'Analyzing Contextual Linking of Heterogeneous Information Models from the Domains BIM and UIM', *ISPRS International Journal of Geo-Information*, vol. 10, no. 12, p. 807 [Online]. DOI: 10.3390/ijgi10120807.

Beetz, J., Pauwels, P., McGlinn, K. and Tormä, S. (2021) 'Linked Data im Bauwesen', in Borrmann, A., König, M., Koch, C. and Beetz, J. (eds) *Building information modeling: Technologische Grundlagen und industrielle Praxis*, 2nd edn, Wiesbaden, Heidelberg, Springer Vieweg, pp. 223–242.

Biljecki, F. and Tauscher, H. (2019) 'Quality of BIM-GIS Conversion', *ISPRS Annals of the Photogrammetry, Remote Sensing and Spatial Information Sciences*, vol. IV-4/W8, pp. 35–42.

Borrmann, A. (2022) 'Building Information Modeling für den Infrastrukturbau', in DVW e.V. and Runder Tisch GIS e.V. (eds) *Leitfaden Geodäsie und BIM: Version 3.1*, Bühl/München, pp. 38–50.

Borrmann, A., König, M., Koch, C. and Beetz, J. (eds). (2021) *Building information modeling: Technologische Grundlagen und industrielle Praxis*, 2nd edn, Wiesbaden, Heidelberg, Springer Vieweg.

Brommer, A., Brückner, I., Ciba, J., Clemen, C., Dönnecke-Herz, C., Eggert, J., Frodl, S., Hüttner, U., Morgner, M., Peter, T., Pucher, A., Raacke, R., Rieß, A. and Röder, D. (2022) *BIM-Klassen der Verkehrswege 2.0: Vorstandardisierungsarbeit der buildingSMART-Fachgruppen Verkehrswege und Landschaftsarchitektur*, 2nd edn, Berlin, bSD Verlag.

Clemen, C. (2022) 'Trends in BIM and GIS standardization – Report from the joint iso/tc59/sc13–iso/tc211 wg: GIS-BIM', *The International Archives of the Photogrammetry, Remote Sensing and Spatial Information Sciences*, vol. XLVI-5/W1-2022, pp. 51–58.

Clemen, C. and Görne, H. (2019) 'Level of Georeferencing (LoGeoRef) using IFC for BIM', vol. 10 [Online]. Available at www.jgcc.geoprevi.ro/docs/2019/10/jgcc_2019_no10_3.pdf.

Clemen, C., Gruner, F. and Pfeifer, J. (2023) 'Infrastrukturdatenhaltung mit BIM und GIS', *DZSF Forschungsberichte*, vol. 46/2023 [Online]. DOI: 10.48755/dzsf.230015.01.

Djuedja, J. F. T., Karray, M. H., Foguem, B. K., Magniont, C. and Abanda, F. H. (2019) 'Interoperability Challenges in Building Information Modelling (BIM)', in Popplewell, K., Thoben, K.-D., Knothe, T. and Poler, R. (eds). *Enterprise Interoperability VIII: Smart Services and Business Impact of Enterprise Interoperability*, Cham, Springer, pp. 275–282.

Donaubauer, A., Kutzner, T., Gruber, U., Borrmann, A. and Krause, K.-U. (2022) 'BIM und GIS-Integration – standardisierte, offene Datenformate', in DVW e.V. and Runder Tisch GIS e.V. (eds). *Leitfaden Geodäsie und BIM: Version 3.1*, Bühl/München, pp. 115–131.

Ellul, C., Stoter, J., Harrie, L., Shariat, M., Behan, A. and Pla, M. (2018) 'Investigating the State of Play of geoBIM Across Europe', in *The International Archives of the Photogrammetry, Remote Sensing and Spatial Information Sciences.* Delft, The Netherlands, Copernicus GmbH, pp. 19–26.

Esser, S. and Borrmann, A. (2021) 'A System Architecture Ensuring Consistency Among Distributed, Heterogeneous Information Models for Civil Infrastructure Projects', *Proceedings of the 13th European Conference on Product and Process Modeling*, Moscow, 2020/2021.

European Commission (2021) *Calculating costs and benefits for the use of Building Information Modeling in public tenders: Methodology handbook* [Online], Luxembourg, Publications Office of the European Union. Available at www.eubim.eu/wp-content/uploads/2021/05/Cost-Benefit-Analysis-for-the-use-of-BIM_user-handbook.pdf.

Fiedler, J. N. (2015) *Modernisierungsszenarien des Baubewilligungsverfahrens unter Berücksichtigung neuer technologischer Hilfsmittel*, Dissertation, Wien, TU Wien.

Fuchs, S. (2015) *Erschließung domänenübergreifender Informationsräume mit Multimodellen* [Online], Dresden, Saechsische Landesbibliothek- Staats- und Universitaetsbibliothek Dresden. Available at www.nbn-resolving.de/urn:nbn:de:bsz:14-qucosa-182126.

Garramone, M., Moretti, N., Scaioni, M., Ellul, C., Re Cecconi, F. and Dejaco, M. C. (2020) 'BIM and GIS Integration for Infrastructure Asset Management a

Bibliometric Analysis', *ISPRS Annals of the Photogrammetry, Remote Sensing and Spatial Information Sciences*, Copernicus GmbH, pp. 77–84.

Gnädinger, J. and Roth, G. (2021) 'Applied Integration of GIS and BIM in Landscape Planning', *Journal of Digital Landscape Architecture*, no. 6-2021, pp. 324–331. *Wichmann Verlag, VDE VERLAG GMBH, Berlin.* http://doi.org/10.14627/537705029

Hausknecht, K. and Liebich, T. (2016) *BIM-Kompendium: Building Information Modeling als neue Planungsmethode* [Online], Stuttgart, Fraunhofer IRB Verlag. Available at www.elibrary.vdi-verlag.de/10.51202/9783816794905.

Häußler, M. and Borrmann, A. (2020) 'Model-Based Quality Assurance in Railway Infrastructure Planning', *Automation in Construction*, vol. 109, p. 102971.

Häußler, M. and Borrmann, A. (2021) 'Knowledge-Based Engineering in the Context of Railway Design by Integrating BIM, BPMN, DMN and the Methodology for Knowledge-Based Engineering Applications (MOKA)', *Journal of Information Technology in Construction*, vol. 26, pp. 193–226.

Herle, S., Becker, R., Wollenberg, R. and Blankenbach, J. (2020) 'GIM and BIM', *PFG – Journal of Photogrammetry, Remote Sensing and Geoinformation Science*, vol. 88, no. 1, pp. 33–42.

ISO (2004) *ISO 19125: ISO 19125-1:2004 Geographic information Simple feature access.*

ISO (2006) *ISO/PAS 26183: ISO/PAS 26183 SASIG Product data quality guidelines for the global automotive industry.*

ISO (2011) *ISO 11354-1: ISO 11354-1 Advanced automation technologies and their applications – Requirements for establishing manufacturing enterprise process interoperability.*

ISO (2012a) *ISO/IEC 19505-2:2012: ISO/IEC 19505-2:2012 Information technology Object Management Group Unified Modeling Language (OMG UML).*

ISO (2012b) *ISO/TS 19150-1: ISO/TS 19150-1 Geoinformation – Ontologie*, Genf: International Standard Organization.

ISO (2014a) *ISO 19101-1: ISO 19101-1:2014 Geographic information Reference model.*

ISO (2014b) *ISO 19115-1: ISO 19115-1:2014 – Geographic information – Metadata.*

ISO (2015) *ISO 19109: ISO 19109 Geoinformation – Regeln zur Erstellung von Anwendungsschemata.*

ISO (2016) *ISO 29481-1: ISO 29481-1:2016 – Building information models Information delivery manual.*

ISO (2018) *ISO 19650-1: ISO 19650-1 – Organization and digitization of information about buildings and civil engineering works, including building information modelling (BIM).*

ISO (2019a) *ISO 10303-42: ISO 10303-42 Industrial automation systems and integration – Product data representation and exchange*, Genf: International Standard Organization.

ISO (2019b) *ISO 19107: ISO 19107:2019 – Geographic information – Spatial schema*, Berlin: Beuth Verlag GmbH.

ISO (2020) *ISO 21597-1:2020: ISO 21597-1:2020 – Information container for linked document delivery Exchange specification*, Berlin: Beuth Verlag GmbH.

ISO (2021) *ISO/TR 23262: ISO/TR 23262:2021 GIS (Geospatial) / BIM-Interoperabilität (ISO/TR 23262:2021)* [Online]. Available at www.iso.org / standard/ 75105.html.

ISO (2022) *ISO 12006-3: ISO 12006-3:2022 Building construction Organization of information about construction works.*

ISO (2023a) *DIN EN ISO 19123-1: ISO 19123-1:2023 – Geographic information Schema for coverage geometry and functions.*

ISO (2023b) *ISO 19157-1:2023: ISO 19157-1:2023 – Geographic information – Data quality.*

ISO (2024a) *16739-1: Industry Foundation Classes (IFC) for data sharing in the construction and facility management industries.*

ISO (2024b) *ISO 7817-1: ISO 7817-1 Building information modelling – Level of information need*, ISO.

Jetlund, K., Onstein, E. and Huang, L. (2020) 'IFC Schemas in ISO/TC 211 Compliant UML for Improved Interoperability between BIM and GIS', *ISPRS International Journal of Geo-Information*, vol. 9, no. 4, p. 278.

Laat, R. de and van Berlo, L. (2011) 'Integration of BIM and GIS: The Development of the CityGML GeoBIM Extension', in Kolbe, T. H., König, G. and Nagel, C. (eds). *Advances in 3D Geo-Information Sciences,* Berlin, Heidelberg, Springer, pp. 211–225.

Liu, X., Wang, X., Wright, G., Cheng, J., Li, X. and Liu, R. (2017) 'A State-of-the-Art Review on the Integration of Building Information Modeling (BIM) and Geographic Information System (GIS)', *ISPRS International Journal of Geo-Information*, vol. 6, no. 2, pp. 53–74 [Online]. DOI: 10.3390/ijgi6020053.

Löwner, M.-O., Gröger, G., Benner, J., Biljecki, F. and Nagel, C. (2016) 'Proposal for a New LOD and Multi-Representation Concept for CityGML', *ISPRS Annals of the Photogrammetry, Remote Sensing and Spatial Information Sciences*, vol. IV-2/W1, pp. 3–12.

Noardo, F., Ellul, C., Harrie, L., Overland, I., Shariat, M., Arroyo Ohori, K. and Stoter, J. (2020) 'Opportunities and Challenges for GeoBIM in Europe: Developing a Building Permits Use-Case to Raise Awareness and Examine Technical Interoperability Challenges', *Journal of Spatial Science*, vol. 65, no. 2, pp. 209–233 [Online]. Available at www.tandfonline.com/doi/full/10.1080/14498596.2019.1627253 (Accessed 15 November 2022).

Noardo, F., Guler, D., Fauth, J., Malacarne, G., Mastrolembo Ventura, S., Azenha, M., Olsson, P.-O. and Senger, L. (2022) 'Unveiling the Actual Progress of Digital Building Permit: Getting Awareness Through a Critical State of the Art Review', *Building and Environment*, vol. 213, p. 108854.

Noardo, F., Harrie, L., Arroyo Ohori, K., Biljecki, F., Ellul, C., Krijnen, T., Eriksson, H., Guler, D., Hintz, D., Jadidi, M. A., Pla, M., Sanchez, S., Soini, V.-P., Stouffs, R., Tekavec, J. and Stoter, J. (2020) 'Tools for BIM-GIS Integration (IFC Georeferencing and Conversions): Results from the GeoBIM Benchmark 2019', *ISPRS International Journal of Geo-Information*, vol. 9, no. 9, p. 502 [Online]. DOI: 10.3390/ijgi9090502.

Pauwels, P., Zhang, S. and Lee, Y.-C. (2017) 'Semantic Web Technologies in AEC Industry: A Literature Overview', *Automation in Construction*, vol. 73, pp. 145–165.

Scherer, R. J. and Schapke, S.-E. (2014) *Informationssysteme im Bauwesen 1,* Berlin, Heidelberg, Springer Berlin Heidelberg.

Taesombut, N. and Chien, A. A. (2007) 'Evaluating Network Information Models on Resource Efficiency and Application Performance in Lambda-Grids', *Proceedings of the 2007 ACM/IEEE conference on Supercomputing – SC '07.* Reno, Nevada, 10.11.2007 – 16.11.2007. New York, New York, USA, ACM Press, pp. 1–12.

USIBD (2019) *Level of Accuracy (LOA) Specification for Building Documentation: Version 3.0* (Document C120). U.S. Institute of Building Documentation (USIBD). https://usibd.org/white-papers-guides/

van Berlo, L., Krijnen, T., Tauscher, H., Liebich, T., van Kranenburg, A. and Paasiala, P. (2021) 'Future of the Industry Foundation Classes: Towards IFC 5', *Proceedings of the 38th International Conference of CIB W78*, pp. 123–134 [Online]. Available at www.itc.scix.net/paper/w78-2021-paper-013.

Wang, H., Pan, Y. and Luo, X. (2019) 'Integration of BIM and GIS in sustainable built environment: A review and bibliometric analysis', *Automation in Construction*, vol. 103, pp. 41–52 [Online]. Available at www.sciencedirect.com/science/article/pii/S0926580518309828.

Wilhelm, L. (2020) *Integration von Building Information Modeling und Umweltplanung am Beispiel der Deutschen Bahn: Masterarbeit Umweltplanung und Ingenieurökologie,* TU München [Online]. Available at www.mediatum.ub.tum.de/doc/1554543/file.pdf.

Zhu, J., Tan, Y., Wang, X. and Wu, P. (2021) 'BIM/GIS Integration for Web GIS-Based Bridge Management', *Annals of GIS*, vol. 27, no. 1, pp. 99–109.

Zobl, F. and Marschallinger, R. (2008) 'GeoBIM – Subsurface Building Information Modelling', *Geoinformatics*, pp. 40–43 [Online]. Available at www.uni-salzburg.elsevierpure.com/de/publications/geobim-subsurface-building-information- modelling.

7

Built-Environment Digital Twins

7.1 Introduction

In Chapter 1, we started with the questions of why digital twins matter and why 3D geospatial information is critical in creating the spatial dimensions of digital twins. In the subsequent chapters, we delved deep into BIM and its integration into GIS. In this final chapter, we expand on the concept of digital twins and explore its various dimensions within the context of built environments. We argue there are parallels between BIM and digital-twins applications but we also make the case that digital twins go well beyond the benefits of BIM, which were presented in Chapter 3.

Built environments are complex and dynamic ecosystems that include multiple stakeholders, diverse data sources, and distinct knowledge domains, such as design, development, and maintenance. Digital twins for built environments are inherently complex, varied, and unpredictable due to the dynamic nature of these environments, which face major changes due to natural events or man-made developments.

Based on the Gemini principles developed by the Centre for Digital Built Britain in 2018, as presented in Figure 7.1, digital twins of built environments offer virtual representations of physical assets, which are accurately updated over time and reflect the real-time behaviour of physical assets (Bolton et al., 2018). The digital twins concept was first coined by NASA, inspired by the sci-fi concept in early 2000, in which NASA used physical twins of spaceships on the ground to test and fix problems that the spacecraft may experience during flights (Glaessgen & Stargel, 2012). Later, industries, supply chains, and manufacturers also started to adopt digital twins in their businesses, services, and processes, enabling specific operations, such as testing, optimisation, and simulation. The Gemini principles identify the key characteristics of digital twins: Having a clear purpose; trustworthy; function effectively for the public good; add value; provide insights; enable security; accessible and open to use; quality; adherence to standards for developing connected

 DOI: 10.1201/9781351200950-7

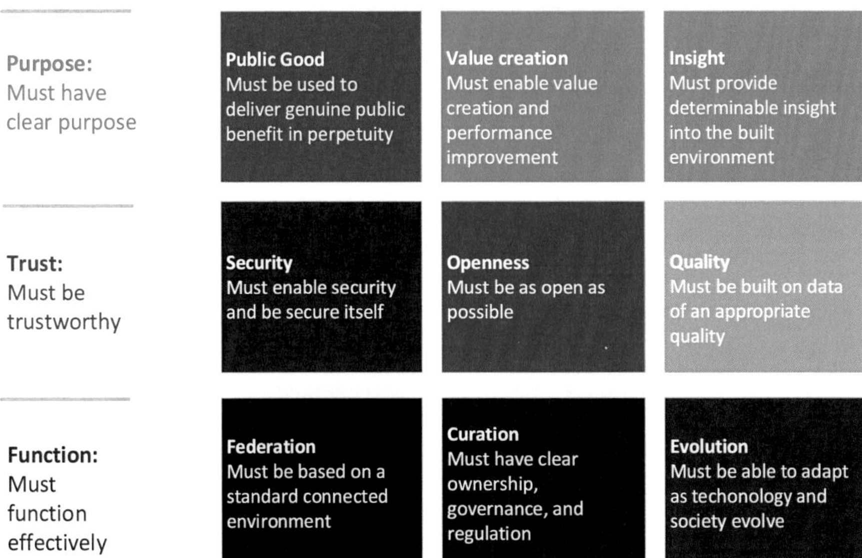

FIGURE 7.1
The Gemini principles for digital twins from the Centre for Digital Built Britain, extracted from Bolton et al. (2018).

environments; clear ownership, governance, and regulation; and adaptable to technological evolutions and advancements (Bolton et al., 2018).

There has recently been increasing interest in developing digital twins and their life cycle from built-environment sectors, more specifically architecture, engineering, and construction (AEC) industries and asset owners (Opoku et al., 2021, 2022; Papadonikolaki et al., 2022). Opoku et al. (2021) provided a comprehensive literature review on the definition of digital twins in various applications, with a focus on AEC sectors. It is worth mentioning that digital twins of built environments are sometimes interchangeably referred to as urban digital twins or city digital twins. In this chapter, for the sake of consistency, we address built-environment digital twins as the overarching concept that includes buildings and infrastructure in urban areas and beyond (Chen et al., 2024; Merino et al., 2023; Papadonikolaki et al., 2022; Petri et al., 2023).

There is currently no universal definition of digital twins and no frameworks for developing one because the definition can be altered for specific applications and scales, depending on the use case, such as transportation, recycling and waste management, water resource management, construction, structural monitoring, planning, infrastructure management,

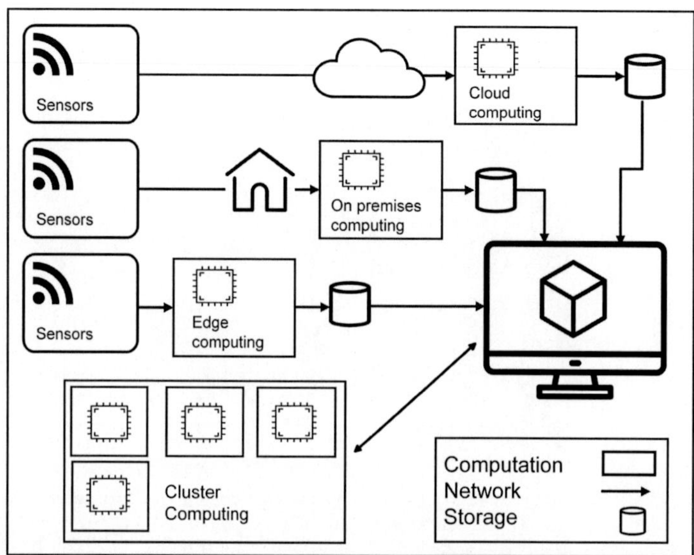

FIGURE 7.2
The typical system architecture of built-environment digital twins. (Adopted from Weil et al., 2023.)

energy efficiency and management, disaster management, and more. However, within the realm of sustainable smart city development, digital twins are considered as city brains to leverage for their modelling, simulation, and forecasting capacities (Weil et al., 2023).

To develop digital twins of built environments, BIM, GIS, and streaming information from the Internet of Things (IoT) and sensors are required. Such diverse and distinct datasets provide digital transformations of built environments into dynamic and up-to-date twin models (Papadonikolaki et al., 2022). Based on Kritzinger et al.'s (2018) literature review, there are three categories of digital twins that are related to the levels of data integration, as follows:

- Digital models, which have no self-driven data interactions between physical objects and digital objects;
- Digital shadows, which have self-driven unidirectional data flows between physical and digital objects;
- Digital twins, which offer bidirectional data integration between existing physical objects and digital objects.

The typical architecture of digital twins is presented in Figure 7.2. This includes computation, network, and data storage. Digital twins require heavy computational capacities due to the increased complexity of BIM and GIS 3D models, as well as the large datasets from sensors and IoT, for which the real-time processing of data is indispensable. Also, the approach of increasing network bandwidth for high-rate large data transmission and real-time application is emergent. Real-time data from sensors, RFID tags, gauges, readers, scanners, cameras, etc., in digital-twins architectures continuously generate huge volumes of unstructured, semi-structured, or structured data. Data transmission is very expensive through cloud servers. To deal with edge computing, collected data need to be pre-processed (Opoku et al., 2021). However, this shortcoming is resolved when 5G technologies are used. On the other hand, the issues of cybersecurity and privacy in digital twins persist. Due to the high volumes of the datasets and their veracity, data storage is an important concern as local, cloud, edge, and cluster computing can serve different purposes (Weil et al., 2023). Different system architectures from computational and data storage perspectives are summarised in Table 7.1.

TABLE 7.1

A typical digital twin system architecture from the computation and data storage perspective. (Adopted from Weil et al., 2023.)

	Definition	**Advantages**	**Limitations**
On-Premises (Local) Computing	Local IT infrastructure and software applications within their own facilities.	- More control over the IT infrastructure and data security. - Customisation of systems to specific needs.	- Expensive to set up and maintain. - Complex and difficult to scale.
Cloud Computing	Delivering internet-based computing resources, such as data storage, processing power, and software.	- Only pay for what is used. - Scalability.	- Expensive for large-scale projects. - Security and privacy concerns.
Edge Computing	Processing data closer to the source of the data rather than in centralised data centres or clouds.	- Reduces data transmission. - Improves the responsiveness of applications. - Cost-effective.	- Challenging to manage and maintain edge devices. - Challenge to ensure data security.
Cluster Computing	Connecting multiple computers together to work as single systems.	- Increased processing power and data storage. - Improves scalability and fault-tolerance of systems.	- Expensive to set up and maintain. - Issues with data consistency and coordination between different nodes.

Indeed, built-environment digital twins is a big data problem, too. As data grow in volume (i.e., the size of the datasets increases), velocity (i.e., the rate of flow), variety (i.e., data from multiple repositories, domains, or types), and veracity (i.e., provenance of the data and its management), the storage, analysis, and visualisation of these data are vital to make the most of the proposed advantages, offering key insights for better and more informed decision-making.

In the context of built-environment digital twins, Lei et al. (2023) identified the following four key aspects in the development of virtual models:

(1) Three-dimensional city models with geometric and semantic information that are provided by BIM and GIS datasets. The most common data formats of GIS data for built environments are CityGML, OGC 3D tiles, indexed 3D scene layers (I3Ss), GeoJSON-LD, CityJASON, KML, and GL transmission format (glTF). Conversely, the most common data formats of BIM data are IFC and the Autodesk family (e.g., Revit, AutoCAD, and Navisworks). These diverse datasets demonstrate the urgent need for data harmonisation (i.e., data fusion) in the development of digital twins into single and consistent platforms, such as graph models (Kiavarz, Jadidi, Rajabifard, et al., 2023; Usmani et al., 2021);

(2) Real-time and near-real-time data that include data from sensors, IoT, RFID tags, gauges, readers, scanners, cameras, etc. This depends on sparse and heterogeneous sensor networks, leading to high temporal and spatial variability;

(3) Capabilities for a variety of operations, e.g., analysing, simulating, and predicting. These processes are mainly run through unidirectional communication instead of bidirectional connections between physical and digital models. More effort is needed to make bidirectional connections that can implement optimisation and manage changes in physical systems;

(4) Capabilities to address social and economic functions in built environments, e.g., enabling participatory processes involving humans as sensors learn about local contexts. This could lead to decision support system implementation, which is an integral part of digital twins. However, it is worth mentioning the necessity for skilled workforces with attributes in the design, development, and maintenance of digital twins, which require diverse knowledge domain expertise as system engineers and developers in AEC sectors.

The application of artificial intelligence (AI), machine learning (ML), and deep learning (DL) algorithms is increasingly critical for providing key insights and automating the processes of developing, updating, and maintaining digital twins. These processes are highly technology-driven and rely on database infrastructure management, IoT, AI, and edge computing to collect and process data (Weil et al., 2023). Also, the immersive visualisation and efficient communication of information are crucial in digital twins development to fulfil its intended goals. With the rise of immersive technology in dashboarding, augmented, virtual, mixed, and extended reality (AR/VR/MR/XR) can provide effective information communication. However, the multiscale, multidimensionality, spatial, and parametric information of built-environment digital twins make them challenging for use in contextualised quantitative visualisation (Weil et al., 2023).

7.2 Life Cycle of Built-Environment Digital Twins

In the context of manufacturing, the life cycle of digital twins is divided into three phases: 1) Design; 2) operation; and 3) service processes. Information related to products is constantly being transferred to virtual models, while the virtual models simulate and validate the scenarios and transmit them to physical entities to optimise design, identify errors, or customise details. There is a connecting loop for information exchange between physical and virtual models (Lei et al., 2023).

Expanding this concept to built environments in the urban context brings more complexity due to the integration of heterogeneous data with physical environments, considering dynamic real-time or near-real-time analysis, which requires a large volume of heterogeneous data, feedback, and high-frequency information flows throughout the life cycle (Papadonikolaki et al., 2022).

As a summary, Lei et al. (2023) divided the life cycle of built-environment digital twins into six phases, as follows and as presented in Figure 7.3:

- Phase 1: Collecting heterogeneous data and defining system architecture and practical values;
- Phase 2: Processing data and determining approaches for data conversion and integration, as well as techniques for developing digital twins;
- Phase 3: Generating physical assets and information flows;
- Phase 4: Managing and disseminating digital twins that refer to visualisation, interoperability, quality, and status;
- Phase 5: Simulating different scenarios and applications to satisfy different use cases;
- Phase 6: Updating and maintaining the digital twins and detecting any changes.

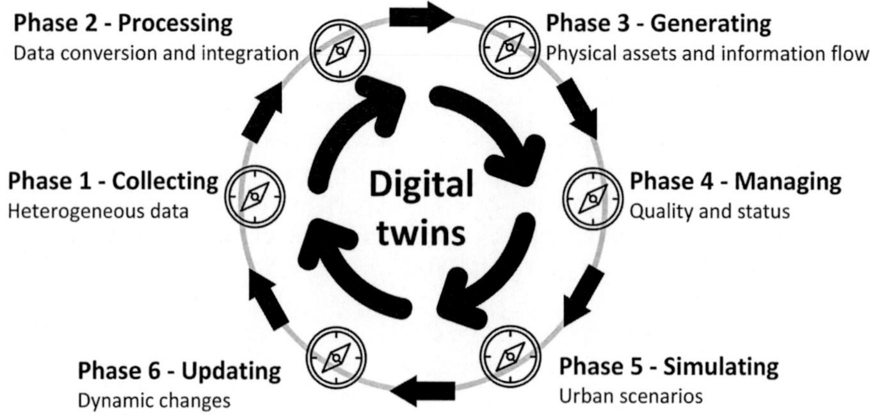

FIGURE 7.3
The typical life cycle of built environment digital twins. (Adapted from Lei et al., 2023.)

These phases include the technical, societal, and legal aspects of the life cycle of digital twins, of which collaboration, data sharing, information, applications, and visualisation lie at the heart.

7.3 Benefits of Built-Environment Digital Twins

Built-environment digital twins provide a variety of benefits in technical, societal, and legal aspects and can lead to better and more sustainable asset planning, design, maintenance and repair scheduling, structural monitoring, and mitigation planning, as well as safety, efficiency, and productivity enhancements.

Since 2018, the study of the adoption of digital twins for built environments has gained huge interest for infrastructure asset management and development within the AEC sector, urban planning, and government organisations. The purposes and benefits of digital twins are broad, covering the visualisation, modelling, and simulation of structure life cycles, facility management, retrofitting and refurbishment planning, space planning, training, safety and risk mitigation, the improved productivity and performance of workforces, and energy efficiency and sustainability (Ammar et al., 2022; Boje et al., 2020; Chen et al., 2024; Coupry et al., 2021; Deng et al., 2021; Deren et al., 2021; Hakimi et al., 2023; Lehner & Dorffner, 2020; Liu et al., 2023; Lu, Parlikad, et al., 2020; Naderi & Shojaei, 2023; Opoku et al., 2022; Petri et al., 2023; Ramonell et al., 2023; Rantanen et al., 2023; Shahinmoghadam et al., n.d.; Weil et al., 2023; Ye et al., 2024).

7.3.1 Digital Twins as Visualisation Tools

Digital twins provide visual representations of information in nD (n-dimensional), beyond 3D model representations, regarding built environments from an immersive and comprehensive perspective (Ammar et al., 2022; Chen et al., 2024; Papadonikolaki et al., 2022; Petri et al., 2023). The representation of nD information is directly related to technological evolutions and use cases and can be defined as follows:

- 3D-Three Dimensions

  This is the geometrical representation of the geographical dimensions (x,y,z) of physical assets. Three-dimensional representations are usually created using BIM data that are integrated with GIS data. They can be used in planning and design before physical assets have been built. This provides an enhanced visualisation perspective for entire projects. Also, 3D visualisations offer a streamlined and transparent communication channel for sharing design expectations, collaborative platforms for multiple stakeholders (regardless of their area of expertise), and the possibility of reduced revision and reworking.
- 4D-Four Dimensions

  This is related to the time component, which includes planning and scheduling during construction and retrofitting projects. It provides improved site planning, optimised scheduling, seamless coordination among stakeholders, and better preparedness, on top of the benefits offered by 3D visualisation.
- 5D-Five Dimensions

  This considers cost estimation, budgetary analysis, and tracking, on top of all of the 4D visualisation attributes. It provides real-time cost visualisation (with notifications of cost changes), automates inventory analysis, and minimises budgetary offshoots due to regular cost reporting.
- 6D-Six Dimensions

  This refers to sustainability measures and energy efficiency visualisation platforms. It can provide transparent platforms for following circular economy and decarbonisation strategies within the AEC sector and built-environment asset management.
- 7D-Seven Dimensions

  This usually refers to facility management and operation information platforms, on top of everything covered by 6D visualisation. It is used to track important asset data for future use, including status, maintenance/operation manuals, warranty information, technical specifications, etc.

Visualisations can be realised through computer-based programs, WebGL-based applications on browsers, or game engine platforms via interactive dashboards and augmented reality, virtual reality, mixed reality, or extended reality (AR/VR/MR/XR) applications.

Digital twins act as visual analytics platforms for the simulation of interactive multiphysics, the modelling of built environments (both discrete and continuous), the generation of what-if scenario, and the life cycle analysis of structures (Ammar et al., 2022; Borrmann et al., 2024; Del Giudice & Osello, 2021; Deng et al., 2021; Deren et al., 2021; Esri, 2024.; Merino et al., 2023; Naserentin et al., 2022; Petri et al., 2023; Rantanen et al., 2023; Relekar et al., 2021). For instance, high-performance simulations, such as those for air quality, computational fluid dynamics (CFD), and urban wind comfort, can be visualised via digital twins platforms (Naserentin et al., 2022).

7.3.2 Digital Twins as Life Cycle Assessment Tools

Digital twins can visualise the entire life cycles of built environments, from raw material extraction, manufacturing and building, transportation, construction, and structure and space management to the demolition of structures at the end of their lives, as well as the recycling and disposal of recovered materials. The literature shows that the vast majority of digital twins are used for structural system integrity, facilities management, monitoring, logistics processes, and energy simulation (Ammar et al., 2022; Deren et al., 2021; Kaewunruen & Xu, 2018; Lin & Cheung, 2020; Lydon et al., 2019; Opoku et al., 2021; Weil et al., 2023) .

7.3.2.1 Digital Twins for Design and Engineering in AEC

Digital twin act as enablers for the design and engineering phases in the AEC sector. As construction projects are developed in a sequence of phases and require constant collaboration from diverse stakeholders, BIM plays an instrumental role in the adoption of digital twins (Ammar et al., 2022). BIM models provide collaborative platforms, allowing data to be added, modified, and verified against real-life scenarios and compliance regulations. This reduces disputes among different stakeholders and encourages automated digital permitting (Chognard et al., 2018). The combination of BIM and sensor information provides designers with complete digital footprints of projects to make informed decisions regarding material selection, energy management, procurement, and supplier selection. All of this leads to a consideration of circular economy and decarbonisation strategies in the AEC sector, in which stakeholders can clarify their purposes and ensure the effective planning, contextual awareness, and understanding of all project stages (Ammar et al., 2022; Opoku et al., 2021). One early work on digital adoption in design and engineering referred to a railway station building project in the UK, for which time, cost, scheduling, and carbon emissions were calculated with renovation assumptions, leading to an economically and environmentally efficient construction project (Kaewunruen & Xu, 2018). In another project, an underground parking garage environment was monitored and managed using a digital twins system (Lin & Cheung, 2020). Another study used digital twins to design thermal systems that were integrated into lightweight roof structures for buildings (Lydon et al., 2019). Clash detection in construction projects is another application that can be facilitated using digital twins (Jiang et al., 2021). In construction management, digital twins provide comprehensive tools that can be enhanced for site preparation, supply chain management and procurement, resource allocation and optimisation, waste management, machinery and equipment management, automated machinery and human–robot interaction and communication, material production and assembly, lean integration, and modular off-site construction applications, to name a few (AlBalkhy et al., 2024; Ammar et al., 2022; Boje et al., 2020; Jiang et al., 2021; Naderi & Shojaei, 2023; Opoku et al., 2021).

7.3.2.2 Digital Twins as Maintenance and Repair Tools

Digital twins also provide platforms for real-time monitoring using as-built models of structures, leading to predictive maintenance, fault detection, state monitoring, and repair planning (Chen et al., 2024; Naderi & Shojaei, 2023; Opoku et al., 2021). Real-time information provides tools to analyse the status of structures in event-based or continuous simulation modes. Digital twins can also improve decision-making via engineering and numerical analyses for monitoring the maturity and mechanical properties of materials, detecting unsafe structural events (such as post-earthquake evaluations), testing loads, investigating the root causes of collapses or damage, etc. (AlBalkhy et al., 2024). For instance, Lu et al. (2020) developed an anomaly detection system using digital twins that identifies diagnostics on the operational condition of assets. This can be used for preventive maintenance and efficient repair planning. In addition, unmanned aerial vehicles (UAVs) and drones equipped with lidar technology and cameras, as well as terrestrial laser scanners, provide excellent source information for structural monitoring applications, such as for bridges, roads, dams, and any other infrastructure (Chen et al., 2024; Macchi et al., 2018).

7.3.2.3 Digital Twins for Energy Efficiency

Digital twins provide simulation, modelling, and data exchange platforms for energy consumption estimation and prescriptive design recommendations for energy-efficient and green building construction and maintenance (Kiavarz, Jadidi, & Esmaili, 2023; Opoku et al., 2021). Another example of an energy efficiency use case is Heathrow Airport in London, as reported in *Digital Twin Toolkit* (Abisogun et al., 2021). The authors simulated different scenarios for energy consumption and identified energy-saving opportunities, such as adjusting HVAC systems and lighting schedules. This led to significant cost savings and reduced environmental impacts.

7.3.2.4 Digital Twins for Refurbishment and Retrofitting Designs

Digital twins can be used to redesign and refurbish existing assets by re-evaluating the performance and condition of designed objects from circular economy and sustainability perspectives (Opoku et al., 2021, 2022). Sustainability and environmental performance can also be considered using digital twins, including thermal design based on occupant comfort, eco-design, the integration of secondary raw materials, construction waste remanufacturing, energy modelling, mapping, and evaluation, and environmental monitoring, to name a few (AlBalkhy et al., 2024). A study in the UK demonstrated how to create digital twins from CAD drawings for existing buildings (Lu, Chen, et al., 2020), providing an accessible method for structures that require monitoring. Digital twins also provide archival and historical platforms for the demolition and retirement of assets, on which the characteristics of demolished assets can be preserved and used in future designs. Digital twins similarly provide tools for heritage building maintenance, such as for reporting the status of damage, choosing materials for repair, studying future structural evolutions for preventive maintenance and practical interventions, as well as understanding documented historical failures of structural components (Angjeliu et al., 2020).

7.3.2.5 Digital Twins for Facility Management, Space Management, and Planning

Digital twins provide real-time and historical portrayals for information and modelling platforms for facility management that can help with space management, light monitoring, occupant comfort, and energy efficiency. For example, what-if analyses and energy simulations allow facility managers to plan the utilisation of space efficiently and improve occupant comfort, as well as decreasing energy consumption (Chen et al., 2024; Lydon et al., 2019; Opoku et al., 2022). Digital twins provide tools for inspection, predictive maintenance, equipment monitoring, and environmental monitoring (e.g., temperature, humidity, air quality, water usage, water quality, etc.), as well as asset condition monitoring. For instance, having digital twins for university campuses could help to facilitate space planning, facility management, flood risk prevention planning, disaster mitigation planning, and much more (Chen et al., 2024; Lu, Parlikad et al., 2020; Ye et al., 2024).

7.3.3 Digital Twins for Safety and Risk Assessment Enhancement

The real-time monitoring of physical assets via sensors, GIS, BIM, and virtual reality (VR) applications allows for early warning systems so that safety risks can be identified (AlBalkhy et al., 2024). This includes safe design and planning, risk prediction and warning, the monitoring and control of worker behaviour, tracking hazardous situations and control actions to avoid accidents, monitoring worker safety, providing disaster management protocols, tracking heavy machinery and providing signals for safe manoeuvring, and indoor safety protocols, to name a few (AlBalkhy et al., 2024). For example, detecting anomalies, such as cracks or shifts, in building structures allows for timely inspections and repairs (Lu, Xie, et al., 2020). The early detection of smoke or abnormal heat patterns makes early fire warnings possible (AlBalkhy et al., 2024). In addition, digital twins simulation platforms can (Lu, Xie, et al., 2020) run different emergency scenarios and choose best practice for crises caused by natural or man-made disasters, including crowd management, resource allocation, and emergency response planning. Furthermore, digital twins can provide excellent platforms for identifying high-risk areas and implementing safety protocols during construction projects (Ammar et al., 2022; Kaewunruen & Xu, 2018; Matar et al., 2017; Papadonikolaki et al., 2022; Petri et al., 2023).

7.3.4 Digital Twins for Workforce Performance Efficiency

Digital twins provide real-time monitoring to capture work progress using IoT, GIS, and BIM for constraints and productivity. This empowers workforces to perform efficiently and confidently by providing risk-free virtual training, running simulations, and using AR/VR/MR/XR to visualise the impacts of decisions. They can simulate scenarios, practice troubleshooting, and learn about system interactions without being involved with physical assets. They can also virtually explore buildings, identify faulty components, and understand maintenance procedures. This allows workforces to confidently diagnose issues faster, thereby reducing downtime during actual repairs. Digital twins also provide access to manuals, schematics, and historical data, further enhancing workforce performance (AlBalkhy et al., 2024).

7.3.5 Digital Twins for Training, Service Enhancement, and Business Growth

Digital twins provide excellent opportunities for training, service enhancement, and business growth among facility managers, planners, and engineers. To be more specific, they offer various applications, from site selection, planning, and city modelling to future designs and user-mirrored adjustments (AlBalkhy et al., 2024; Petri et al., 2023). For instance, Singapore's Smart Nation Initiative is an example of a system that not only enhances services but also provides valuable learning experiences for professionals across different domains within built environments. Digital twins of the entire city were developed, including buildings, infrastructure, and transportation networks, to provide simulations and AR/VR applications, such as optimising traffic flows, enhancing emergency response systems, improving flood protection planning, and much more (The Institution of Engineering Technology, 2023). Digital twins provide interactive and intuitive platforms for urban planners to gain hands-on experience in managing complex urban environments, making informed decisions, and understanding the impacts of various interventions before implementing them. All of this contributes towards training experts to embed resiliency and sustainability into each step of their designs, construction, and operations.

7.4 Challenges in Developing Built-Environment Digital Twins

Lei et al. (2023) developed a typology of identified technical challenges for built-environment digital twins, following Delphi survey methods. Among the technical challenges identified in multiple studies were difficulties with data quality (e.g., accuracy, availability, and information loss), data standards (e.g., top-level design and inconsistent adaptation), interoperability (e.g., data conversion and software incompatibility), data integration (e.g., heterogeneous techniques and incompatible systems), data complexity, (e.g., dynamic activity and versatile information), software (e.g., licensing issues), hardware (e.g., connectivity), and updating/versioning (e.g., version management, latency, and costs) (Chen et al., 2024; Lei et al., 2023; Merino et al., 2023; Naserentin et al., 2022; Opoku et al., 2021, 2022; Rantanen et al., 2023; Singh et al., 2021; Weil et al., 2023). There was also a vast list of non-technical challenges, which included problems with sensitivity (e.g., security hierarchy and regulation), collaboration (e.g., co-creation mechanisms and workflows), ownership (e.g., data sharing and access frameworks), trustworthiness and reliability, participation (e.g., uneven access and participatory feedback), financing (e.g., equipment, computation, and human resources costs), capacity building (e.g., knowledge domain experts and skillsets), and understanding (e.g., the definition of digital twins) (Chen et al., 2024; Lei et al., 2023; Merino et al., 2023; Naserentin et al., 2022; Opoku et al., 2021, 2022; Rantanen et al., 2023; Singh et al., 2021; Weil et al., 2023). A summary of the identified technical and non-technical challenges is presented in Figure 7.4.

Data sharing procedures and the exchange of millions of assets in digital twins of built environments need to be usable by sub-contractors, IoT device manufacturers, and facilities managers, all of whom would use digital twins in different ways and would need to connect them to ever wider sets of data. This requires the development of a common understanding of digital twins, backed by a common language, commercial and contractual models, security and privacy strategies, interoperability (including data models and APIs), and adapted behaviours and cultures to encourage new, digitally enabled practices. Interoperability is among the biggest challenges in

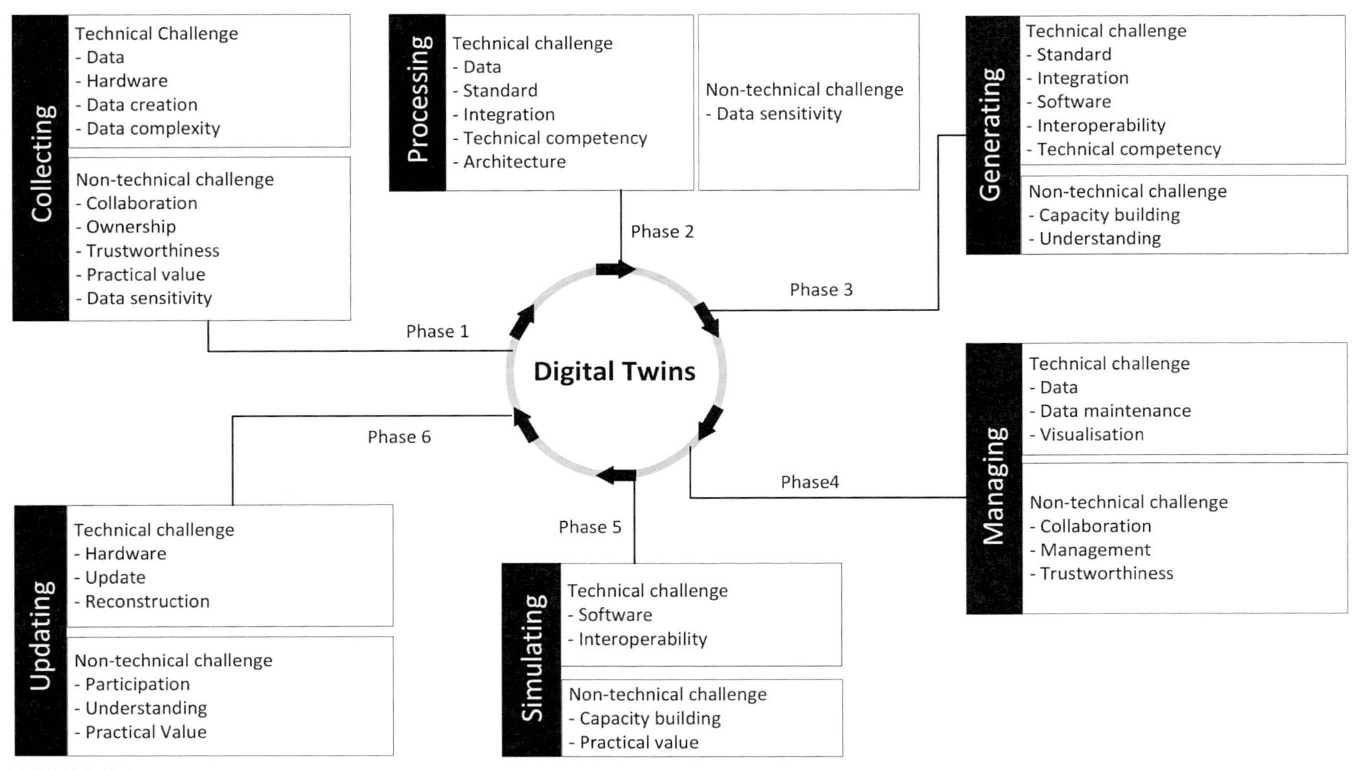

FIGURE 7.4
Identified technical and non-technical challenges according to each phase of the digital twins life cycle. (Adopted from Lei et al., 2023.)

built-environment digital twins that have been discussed in the literature, while data conversion between BIM and GIS has also been considered. BIM and GIS integration traditionally follows either IFC-to-CityGML or IFC-to-shapefile workflows (or vice versa); however, such conversions are complex, leading to the loss of information (Halbout et al., 2023; A. E. H. Hor et al., 2018; A.-H. Hor et al., 2016; Noardo et al., 2020; Usmani et al., 2020). This could be due to the encoding, semantics, geometries, coordinate reference systems, or topological components of the data involved (Noardo et al., 2020).

To deal with the challenges in both the technical and non-technical domains, specific solutions are required. For instance, semantic graph technology and graph structures are promising solutions for tackling issues with interoperability, data complexity, data standards, and data integration (Halbout et al., 2023; A. E. H. Hor et al., 2018; A.-H. Hor et al., 2016; Kiavarz, Jadidi, Rajabifard, et al., 2023; Noardo et al., 2020; Usmani et al., 2020, 2021). As another example, hierarchical data-sharing that enable important collaboration between stakeholders would be ideal for dealing with issues of digital twins ownership due to their degree of sensitivity and availability (Lei et al., 2023).

On the other hand, the ethical, legal, and social aspects of the development of built-environment digital twins have garnered interest in rigorous studies on data privacy, inclusivity, transparency, and social perception (Weil et al., 2023), including the following components:

- Citizen privacy and cybersecurity (data privacy);
- Data sharing and digital twins-based tools (transparency);
- Citizen engagement, choice of information communication, tools with accessibility features for people with disabilities (inclusivity); and
- Developers bias in socioeconomic environments, leading to the lack of cultural diversity (social perception).

7.5 Existing Platforms and Technologies

In general, several technologies related to data, high-fidelity modelling, and model-based simulation can be used for digital twins development. Developing digital twins from existing structures has become more feasible due to the rapid advancements in 3D surveying technologies and the adoption of BIM as a mandate by many countries for newly built structures. Lidar and laser scanner data (as point clouds) are the most common types of raw data for the creation of 3D models for digital twins. Imagery and sensor information also provide geometrical and

TABLE 7.2

A summary of existing platforms and technologies for the development of digital twins and the maintenance of built environments. (Adopted from Jiang et al., 2021.)

Digital Twins Implementation	Technologies and Software
Digitalisation/Transformation of Assets	In-house programming, Revit, AutoCAD, smart phone applications, Navisworks, Leica Cyclone REGISTER 360, Graphisoft ArchiCAD, Rhino, ArcGIS, Autodesk Recap, CloudCompare, finite element models, SketchUp, Unity3D, AR&VR, Bentley, Ecotect EnergyPlus, RealWorkSurvey, xBIM, 3ds Max, Faro Scene, Solibri, and many more.
Connected Networks and Related Technologies	Sensors, laser scanners, lidar, cameras, mobile phones/ tablets/mobile devices, Wlan/WiFi, actuators, GPS/ GNSS/satellites, photogrammetry, thermal imaging, Bluetooth, RFID, surveys, remote sensing, total stations, PDA, robots, 3G/4G/GSM/UHF, QR codes, radars, RTLS, ultrasonic, LAN, optical scanning, radars, and COBie,
Data Types and Formats	2D drawings, BIM (IFC) data as Revit format, GIS data, CityGML, OGC 3D tiles, indexed 3D scene layers (I3Ss), GeoJSON-LD, CityJASON, KML, GL transmission format (glTF), images, thermal images, GPS or GNSS data, RFID data, survey data, las/xyz lidar data, semantic information, historical maps, and geological survey data,
Virtual Visualisation	In-house programming, webGL, Unity Game Engine, City Engine, augmented/virtual/mixed/extended reality platforms, interactive dashboards in Power BI, and Caesium.
Service Functions	Management, visualisation, monitoring, detection, calculation, analysis, simulation, decision-making, estimation, automatic control, optimisation, diagnosis, retrofitting, prognostics, navigation, clash detection, tracking, and training.
Examples of Companies Offering Digital Twins	City Engine (ESRI)[1], Dalux[2], iTwin (Bentley)[3], VIM (PowerBI-based system)[4], Unity Game Engine (Unity)[5], Archidata[6], intelligent network solutions (INSs)[7], Azur Digital Twins Platform[8], and many more.

non-geometrical information for the development of digital twins (Chen et al., 2024; Jiang et al., 2021; Lenart et al., 2018; Lu, Parlikad et al., 2020). Table 7.2 summarises the diverse technologies that have been used for the development of digital twins in the AEC sector and smart cities contexts, according to the global literature. The table highlights the most commonly used digital transformations of asset technologies, related technologies for building connected networks, supported data types and formats, and the variety of service functions that digital twins offer. This list was prepared based on literature reviews and the authors' experiences with different platforms. We disclose here that this list could be much larger due to the high rate of technological evolution; however, we prepared this list based on an extensive literature review.

7.6 Summary

Built-environment digital twins have attracted widespread attention, not only in research and governmental communities but also in AEC industry sectors, for their ability to facilitate better, sustainable, and informed decision-making about the planning, design, construction, maintenance, and operation of built environments. The significant realisation of research, developments, and innovations in digital twins could lead to remarkable benefits for built environments, for which efficiency and sustainability are the main goals. However, these are only possible if multiple digital twins can communicate with each other and work together on an urban scale. Encouraging various stakeholders and organisations to agree on a shared view of what digital twins look like, both commercially and technologically, is a vital step towards the successful adoption of digital twins for built environments and the realisation of their benefits. However, there is still a lack of understanding surrounding the definition, value, and necessity of this technology in making built environments more resilient and sustainable. The technological development of digital twins is advancing fast. However, the inclusion of AI, AR/VR, and robotics in the life cycle of digital twins is an emergent topic to be considered in the next decade if we are to achieve Industry 4.0 completely. It is worth mentioning that the development of digital twins is a multi/transdisciplinary domain that requires new skills on top of knowledge domain expertise, including the mastery of digital transformation, programming, and the virtualisation of spaces in immersive environments (such as AR/VR/MR/XR platforms), as well as the utilisation of machine learning, deep learning, and AI in AEC sectors and urban planning in academic, government, and private sectors.

Notes

1 www.esri.com/en-us/digital-twin/overview
2 www.dalux.com/en-ca/
3 www.bentley.com/software/itwin-platform/
4 www.vimaec.com
5 https://unity.com/solutions/digital-twin-simulation
6 https://archidata.com/en/index
7 www.ins.com.mk
8 https://azure.microsoft.com/en-in/products/digital-twins/

Bibliography

Abisogun, B., Bailey, J., Callcut, M., Curtis, P., Dobos, J., Evans, S., Henderson, T., Kidd, B., Lake, J., McMillan, L., Mills, L., Miskimmin, I., Oren, R., Rutland, C., Sapherson, H., Tuffour, A., van Manen, P., Varga, L., & Winfield, M. (2021). *Digital Twin Toolkit:* Developing the business case for your digital twin Report, University of Cambridge (access via www.cdbb.cam.ac.uk/news/dt-toolkit-making-business-case-dt).

AlBalkhy, W., Karmaoui, D., Ducoulombier, L., Lafhaj, Z., & Linner, T. (2024). Digital twins in the built environment: Definition, applications, and challenges. *Automation in Construction, 162,* 105368. https://doi.org/10.1016/j.autcon.2024.105368

Ammar, A., Nassereddine, H., AbdulBaky, N., AbouKansour, A., Tannoury, J., Urban, H., & Schranz, C. (2022). Digital twins in the construction industry: A perspective of practitioners and building authority. *Frontiers in Built Environment, 8.* https://doi.org/10.3389/fbuil.2022.834671

Angjeliu, G., Coronelli, D., & Cardani, G. (2020). Development of the simulation model for digital twin applications in historical Masonry buildings: The integration between numerical and experimental reality. *Computers and Structures, 238.* https://doi.org/10.1016/j.compstruc.2020.106282

Boje, C., Guerriero, A., Kubicki, S., & Rezgui, Y. (2020). Towards a semantic construction digital twin: Directions for future research. In *Automation in Construction* (Vol. 114). Elsevier B.V. https://doi.org/10.1016/j.autcon.2020.103179

Bolton, A., Butler, L., Dabson, I., et al., & CDBB. (2018). *The Gemini principles.* University of Cambridge. https://doi.org/10.17863/CAM.32260

Borrmann, A., Biswanath, M., Braun, A., Chen, Z., Cremers, D., Heeramaglore, M., Hoegner, L., Mehranfar, M., Kolbe, T. H., Petzold, F., Rueda, A., Solonets, S., & Zhu, X. X. (2024). *Pre-print Artificial Intelligence for the automated creation of multi-scale digital twins of the built world-AI4TWINNING.* Recent Advances in 3D Geoinformation Science. 3DGeoInfo 2023. Lecture Notes in Geoinformation and Cartography. Springer, Cham. https://doi.org/10.1007/978-3-031-43699-4_14

Chen, G., Alomari, I., Taffese, W. Z., Shi, Z., Afsharmovahed, M. H., Mondal, T. G., & Nguyen, S. (2024). Multifunctional models in digital and physical twinning of the built environment—A University campus case study. *Smart Cities, 7*(2), 836–858. https://doi.org/10.3390/smartcities7020035

Chognard, S., Dubois, A., Benmansour, Y., Torri, E., & Domer, B. (2018). Digital construction permit: A round trip between GIS and IFC. *Lecture Notes in Computer Science (Including Subseries Lecture Notes in Artificial Intelligence and Lecture Notes in Bioinformatics), 10864 LNCS.* https://doi.org/10.1007/978-3-319-91638-5_16

Coupry, C., Noblecourt, S., Richard, P., Baudry, D., & Bigaud, D. (2021). BIM-Based digital twin and XR devices to improve maintenance procedures in smart buildings: A literature review. In *Applied Sciences (Switzerland)* (Vol. 11, Issue 15). MDPI AG. https://doi.org/10.3390/app11156810

Del Giudice, M., & Osello, A. (2021). *Handbook of research on developing smart cities based on digital twins.* IGI Global, Engineering Science Reference an imprint of IGI Global.

Deng, M., Menassa, C. C., & Kamat, V. R. (2021). From BIM to digital twins: A systematic review of the evolution of intelligent building representations in the AEC-FM industry. *Journal of Information Technology in Construction, 26,* 58–83. https://doi.org/10.36680/J.ITCON.2021.005

Deren, L., Wenbo, Y., & Zhenfeng, S. (2021). Smart city based on digital twins. *Computational Urban Science*, *1*(1). https://doi.org/10.1007/s43762-021-00005-y

Esri. (2024). *ArcGIS: The foundation for digital twins creating the sustainable infrastructure of the future*. ESRI Publication (e-Book).

Glaessgen, E. H., & Stargel, D. S. (2012). The digital twin paradigm for future NASA and U.S. air force vehicles. *53rd AIAA/ASME/ASCE/AHS/ASC Structures, Structural Dynamics and Materials Conference: Special Session on the Digital Twin*, 1818.

Hakimi, O., Liu, H., & Abudayyeh, O. (2023). Digital twin-enabled smart facility management: A bibliometric review. In *Frontiers of Engineering Management*. Higher Education Press Limited Company. https://doi.org/10.1007/s42524-023-0254-4

Halbout, H., Robida, F., & Jadidi, M. (2023). BIM, GIS, 3D modeling: Complementarity / convergence / digital continuity. In E. S. I.-T. Collections classiques (Ed.), *BIM Shared Modeling, Shared Data, the New Art of Building* (1st ed., Vol. 1, pp. 181–207). ISTE.

Hor, A. E. H., Gunho, S., Claudio, P., Jadidi, M., & Afnan, A. (2018). A semantic graph database for BIM-GIS integrated information model for an intelligent urban mobility web. *ISPRS Annals of Photogrammetry, Remote Sensing and Spatial Information Sciences*, *IV*(October), 1–5.

Hor, A.-H., Jadidi, A., & Sohn, G. (2016). BIM-GIS integrated geospatial information model using semantic Web and RDF graphs. *ISPRS Annals of Photogrammetry, Remote Sensing & Spatial Information Sciences*, *3*(4), 73–79. https://doi.org/10.5194/isprsannals-III-4-73-2016

The Institution of Engineering Technology (2023). *Digital twins for the built environment*. The Institution of Engineering Technology Report, ATKINS member of SNC-Lavalin Group (theiet.org/built-environment)

Jiang, F., Ma, L., Broyd, T., & Chen, K. (2021). Digital twin and its implementations in the civil engineering sector. In *Automation in Construction* (Vol. 130). Elsevier B.V. https://doi.org/10.1016/j.autcon.2021.103838

Kaewunruen, S., & Xu, N. (2018). Digital twin for sustainability evaluation of railway station buildings. *Frontiers in Built Environment*, *4*. https://doi.org/10.3389/fbuil.2018.00077

Kiavarz, H., Jadidi, M., & Esmaili, P. (2023). A graph-based explanatory model for room-based energy efficiency analysis based on BIM data. *Frontiers in Built Environment*, *9*. https://doi.org/10.3389/fbuil.2023.1256921

Kiavarz, H., Jadidi, M., Rajabifard, A., & Sohn, G. (2023). An automated space-based graph generation framework for building energy consumption estimation. *Buildings*, *13*(2). https://doi.org/10.3390/buildings13020350

Kritzinger, W., Karner, M., Traar, G., Henjes, J., & Sihn, W. (2018). Digital Twin in manufacturing: A categorical literature review and classification. *IFAC-PapersOnLine*, *51*(11), 1016–1022. https://doi.org/10.1016/j.ifacol.2018.08.474

Lehner, H., & Dorffner, L. (2020). Digital geoTwin Vienna: Towards a digital twin city as Geodata hub. *PFG – Journal of Photogrammetry, Remote Sensing and Geoinformation Science*, *88*(1), 63–75. https://doi.org/10.1007/s41064-020-00101-4

Lei, B., Janssen, P., Stoter, J., & Biljecki, F. (2023). Challenges of urban digital twins: A systematic review and a Delphi expert survey. In *Automation in Construction* (Vol. 147). Elsevier B.V. https://doi.org/10.1016/j.autcon.2022.104716

Lenart, S., Janjić, V., Jovanović, U., Vezočnik, R., Simo-Serra, E., Iizuka, S., Sasaki, K., Ishikawa, H., October, B., Huang, W., Olsson, P. O., Kanters, J., Harrie, L., McArthur, J. J., Shahbazi, N., Fok, R., Raghubar, C., Bortoluzzi, B., An, A., … Schooling, J. (2018). A review of building information modeling (BIM) and the internet of things (IoT) devices integration: Present status and future trends. *Automation in Construction*, *101*(1), 127–139. https://doi.org/10.1016/j.autcon.2019.01.020

Lin, Y.-C., & Cheung, W.-F. (2020). Developing WSN/BIM-based environmental monitoring management system for parking garages in smart cities. *Journal of Management in Engineering*, *36*(3), 4020012. https://doi.org/10.1061/(ASCE)ME.1943-5479.0000760

Liu, C., Zhang, P., & Xu, X. (2023). Literature review of digital twin technologies for civil infrastructure. *Journal of Infrastructure Intelligence and Resilience*, *2*(3), 100050. https://doi.org/10.1016/j.iintel.2023.100050

Lu, Q., Chen, L., Li, S., & Pitt, M. (2020). Semi-automatic geometric digital twinning for existing buildings based on images and CAD drawings. *Automation in Construction*, *115*. https://doi.org/10.1016/j.autcon.2020.103183

Lu, Q., Parlikad, A. K., Woodall, P., Don Ranasinghe, G., Xie, X., Liang, Z., Konstantinou, E., Heaton, J., & Schooling, J. (2020). Developing a digital twin at building and city levels: Case study of West Cambridge Campus. *Journal of Management in Engineering*, *36*(3). https://doi.org/10.1061/(asce)me.1943-5479.0000763

Lu, Q., Xie, X., Parlikad, A. K., & Schooling, J. M. (2020). Digital twin-enabled anomaly detection for built asset monitoring in operation and maintenance. *Automation in Construction*, *118*. https://doi.org/10.1016/j.autcon.2020.103277

Lydon, G. P., Caranovic, S., Hischier, I., & Schlueter, A. (2019). Coupled simulation of thermally active building systems to support a digital twin. *Energy and Buildings*, *202*. https://doi.org/10.1016/j.enbuild.2019.07.015

Macchi, M., Roda, I., Negri, E., & Fumagalli, L. (2018). Exploring the role of digital twin for asset lifecycle management. *IFAC-PapersOnLine*, *51*(11), 790–795. https://doi.org/10.1016/j.ifacol.2018.08.415

Matar, M., Osman, H., Georgy, M., Abou-Zeid, A., & El-Said M. (2017). A systems engineering approach for realizing sustainability in infrastructure Projects. *HBRC Journal*, *13*(2), 190–201, ISSN 1687-4048, https://doi.org/10.1016/j.hbrcj.2015.04.005.

Merino, J., Moretti, N., Xie, X., Chang, J. Y., & Parlikad, A. (2023). Data integration for digital twins in the built environment based on federated data models. *Proceedings of the Institution of Civil Engineers: Smart Infrastructure and Construction*, *176*(4), 194–211. https://doi.org/10.1680/jsmic.23.00002

Naderi, H., & Shojaei, A. (2023). Digital twinning of civil infrastructures: Current state of model architectures, interoperability solutions, and future prospects. In *Automation in Construction* (Vol. 149). Elsevier B.V. https://doi.org/10.1016/j.autcon.2023.104785

Naserentin, V., Somanath, S., Eleftheriou, O., & Logg, A. (2022). Combining open source and commercial tools in digital twin for cities generation. *IFAC-PapersOnLine*, *55*(11), 185–189. https://doi.org/10.1016/j.ifacol.2022.08.070

Noardo, F., Harrie, L., Ohori, K. A., Biljecki, F., Ellul, C., Krijnen, T., Eriksson, H., Guler, D., Hintz, D., Jadidi, M. A., Pla, M., Sanchez, S., Soini, V. P., Stouffs, R., Tekavec, J., & Stoter, J. (2020). Tools for BIM-GIS integration (IFC georeferencing and conversions): Results from the GeoBIM benchmark 2019. *ISPRS International Journal of Geo-Information*, *9*(9). https://doi.org/10.3390/ijgi9090502

Opoku, D. G. J., Perera, S., Osei-Kyei, R., & Rashidi, M. (2021). Digital twin application in the construction industry: A literature review. In *Journal of Building Engineering* (Vol. 40). Elsevier Ltd. https://doi.org/10.1016/j.jobe.2021.102726

Opoku, D. G. J., Perera, S., Osei-Kyei, R., Rashidi, M., Famakinwa, T., & Bamdad, K. (2022). Drivers for digital twin adoption in the construction industry: A systematic literature review. In *Buildings* (Vol. 12, Issue 2). MDPI. https://doi.org/10.3390/buildings12020113

Papadonikolaki, E., Krystallis, I., & Morgan, B. (2022). Digital technologies in built environment projects: Review and future directions. *Project Management Journal, 53*(5), 501–519. https://doi.org/10.1177/87569728211070225

Petri, I., Rezgui, Y., Ghoroghi, A., & Alzahrani, A. (2023). Digital twins for performance management in the built environment. *Journal of Industrial Information Integration, 33*. https://doi.org/10.1016/j.jii.2023.100445

Ramonell, C., Chacón, R., & Posada, H. (2023). Knowledge graph-based data integration system for digital twins of built assets. *Automation in Construction, 156*. https://doi.org/10.1016/j.autcon.2023.105109

Rantanen, T., Julin, A., Virtanen, J. P., Hyyppä, H., & Vaaja, M. T. (2023). Open geospatial data integration in game engine for urban digital twin applications. *ISPRS International Journal of Geo-Information, 12*(8). https://doi.org/10.3390/ijgi12080310

Relekar, A., Smolira, P., Petrova, E., & Svidt, K. (2021). Enabling Digital Twins with Advanced Visualization and Contextualization of Sensor Data with BIM and Web Technologies. *Proceedings of the 38th CIB W78 conference on Information and Communication Technologies for AECO*. Luxembourg, www.cibw78-ldac-2021.lu/

Shahinmoghadam, M., Motamedi, A., Ca, A. M., & Cheriet, M. (n.d.). *Applying Machine Learning and Digital Twinning for the Live Assessment of Thermal Comfort in Buildings*.

Singh, S., Shehab, E., Higgins, N., Fowler, K., Reynolds, D., Erkoyuncu, J. A., & Gadd, P. (2021). Data management for developing digital twin ontology model. *Proceedings of the Institution of Mechanical Engineers, Part B: Journal of Engineering Manufacture, 235*(14), 2323–2337. https://doi.org/10.1177/0954405420978117

Usmani, A. U., Jadidi, M., & Sohn, G. (2020). Automatic ontology generation of BIM and GIS data. *International Archives of the Photogrammetry, Remote Sensing and Spatial Information Sciences – ISPRS Archives, 43*(B4), 77–80. https://doi.org/10.5194/isprs-archives-XLIII-B4-2020-77-2020

Usmani, A. U., Jadidi, M., & Sohn, G. (2021). Towards the automatic ontology generation and alignment of BIM and GIS data formats. *ISPRS Annals of the Photogrammetry, Remote Sensing and Spatial Information Sciences, 8*(4/W2-2021), 183–188. https://doi.org/10.5194/isprs-annals-VIII-4-W2-2021-183-2021

Weil, C., Bibri, S. E., Longchamp, R., Golay, F., & Alahi, A. (2023). Urban digital twin challenges: A systematic review and perspectives for sustainable smart cities. *Sustainable Cities and Society, 99*. https://doi.org/10.1016/j.scs.2023.104862

Ye, X., Jamonnak, S., Van Zandt, S., Newman, G., & Suermann, P. (2024). Developing campus digital twin using interactive visual analytics approach. *Frontiers of Urban and Rural Planning*, 2(1), 9. https://doi.org/10.1007/s44243-024-00033-2

Index

For Product Safety Concerns and Information please contact our EU representative GPSR@taylorandfrancis.com Taylor & Francis Verlag GmbH, Kaufingerstraße 24, 80331 München, Germany